Youth and Media

WARSAW STUDIES IN CULTURE AND SOCIETY

Edited by Jacek Wasilewski

Vol. 3

Mirosław Filiciak
Michał Danielewicz
Mateusz Halawa
Paweł Mazurek
Agata Nowotny

Youth and Media

New Media and
Cultural Participation

Bibliographic Information published by the Deutsche Nationalbibliothek
The Deutsche Nationalbibliothek lists this publication in the Deutsche Nationalbibliografie; detailed bibliographic data is available in the internet at http://dnb.d-nb.de.

Cover Design: © Olaf Gloeckler, Atelier Platen, Friedberg

This publication was funded by the Ministry of Science and Higher Education of the Polish Republic National Programme for the Development of Humanities.

 NARODOWY PROGRAM ROZWOJU HUMANISTYKI

Library of Congress Cataloging-in-Publication Data

Filiciak, Miroslaw.
  Youth and media : new media and cultural participation / Miroslaw Filiciak, Michal Danielewicz, Mateusz Halawa, Pawel Mazurek, Agata Nowotny.
    pages cm. — (Warsaw studies in culture and society ; vol. 3)
  ISBN 978-3-631-62331-2
  1. Internet and teenagers—Poland. 2. Social media—Poland. 3. Poland—Social life and customs. I. Title.
  HQ799.2.I5F55 2013
  004.67'80835—dc23
                                                          20130115788

ISSN 2192-4961
ISBN 978-3-631-62331-2

© Peter Lang GmbH
Internationaler Verlag der Wissenschaften
Frankfurt am Main 2013
All rights reserved.
PL Academic Research is an Imprint of Peter Lang GmbH.

Peter Lang – Frankfurt am Main · Bern · Bruxelles · New York · Oxford · Warszawa · Wien

All parts of this publication are protected by copyright. Any utilisation outside the strict limits of the copyright law, without the permission of the publisher, is forbidden and liable to prosecution. This applies in particular to reproductions, translations, microfilming, and storage and processing in electronic retrieval systems.

www.peterlang.de

Table of contents

"Youth and media" report 9
Foreword to English edition 13
Introduction: Remediation 17

INTRODUCTION:
Connected and online, the ethnography of a digital world 27
A new existential situation 27
Melded to media, participating in culture 28
Ethnography of new media 29
Ethnography in a database 30
    How we worked? 32
    How to read this report? 35

BEING TOGETHER 37
    At the 18th birthday party 42
The power of close bonds 46
    Black boxes, or material culture in the new media era, *Marek Krajewski* 47

INTENSITY 51
Coordination of face to face and hand in hand meetings 53
    Constant stand-by, *Marek Krajewski* 54
New dimensions of contacts 57
To be is to take photos 59
    Photographic sociability and remediating memory, *José van Dijk* 62

LOVE 65
Love in the age of digital media 67
An asymmetric balance 68
Getting closer while apart 69
Romantic artifacts 69
    An intimate internet 71

TECHNOLOGIES OF REFLEXIVITY 73
Trading attention, or how social networks materialize glances 75
    Aestheticizing the everyday, or why life must have a vibe 78
Reflexive travel in the archives of togetherness 81
'The self' in a relationship network 82
    Robert. Facebook and politics 83
Successfully being yourself 86
    Digital technologies and the technologies of the self, *Małgorzata Jacyno* 87

Reflexively being yourself among others 92
Searching for proof of one's existence, *Mirosława Marody* 93

SHARING 99
C, like co-internet 104
The rules of sharing 107
Co-internet 110

GEEKING OUT. PASSIONS IN THE NETWORKED ERA 113
Last.fm: vibes via an algorithm 119
A never ending gallery opening 124
Digart: community of practices, online studio 126
Greniu. Listening and making music 129
History – networked 133
A town's visual archive 135
A history seen on the Web 136
Majka: a hypothesis about learning shortcuts 137
Cultural omnivorousness? *Małgorzata Jacyno* 139

AT SCHOOL 145
Media under the desk 147
Rapidshare *Iliad* 148
Rule of the algorithm 149
...That's when i ask uncle Google 151
Anyone can write, anyone can correct 152
Educational WWW 153
School outside of school 155
Two clicks away from distraction 157
Text message test 158
Student – teacher: relations mediated by media 160
Schools and new media, *Tomasz Szkudlarek* 161

MAL DU SIÈCLE? *Zygmunt Bauman* 165

NEW QUESTIONS ABOUT CULTURAL PARTICIPATION 173
Żuku: no longer a consumer, not yet a creator 175
Henry Jenkins: new forms of cultural participation 177
Wiesław Godzic: television's end, creativity's beginning 178
Wojciech J. Burszta: describing a revolution 181
An "insert" identity 182
Culture as relations with content, not institutions 183
Marek Krajewski: expiration 185

(SEE) *Tomek Ratter* 193

Acknowledgments 209
Additional thanks to: 209
Bibliography 211
Notes on contributors 213

"Youth and media" report

Is an ethnographic description of the daily life of youths growing up in a world of digital technologies.

This report is the culmination of a year-long research project carried out by the Popular Culture Research Center of the University of Social Sciences and Humanities in Warsaw for the Ministry of Culture and National Heritage under the leadership of Dr. Mirosław Filiciak. The nine-person team of media studies experts, sociologists and anthropologists was tasked with illustrating the way in which new technologies are impacting the lives of young people in Poland. The project's key component was a two week period of ethnographic fieldwork carried out in August and September, during which researchers studied the lives of high school students in three Polish cities. During meetings, interviews, trips and parties, they met and spoke with 137 young people. The high school students showed the ethnographers their world and spoke about daily life in the era of digital media and networked communication.

This report is structured around chapters which address key dimensions of these young people's daily lives: "Being Together," "Love," "Geeking Out," and "At School," as well as chapters which focus on analytical categories significant in understanding the cultural environment co-created by new media: "Intensity," "Technologies of Reflectivity," and "Sharing."

In the first chapter – "Being Together" – we show the primacy of face to face contacts. Meeting up, hanging out, group trips, nights on the town, sitting on a park bench and talking are the most significant types of interactions. New technologies are used to coordinate these get-togethers, mediate contacts when they become impossible (for example: after returning home from school) and maintain the experience of closeness.

The second chapter – "Intensity" – looks closely at how young people who are melded to their media-objects use the ability to remain in constant contact, coordination and representation. We show how everyday life becomes more intensive as the technologies of tele-availability and tele-presence drive their users into a unique state of vigilance. The physical sphere of a face to face conversation is interwoven with communication networks which allow a partial surpassing of time-space limits of social lives. The effect is an experience of connectedness and online access – an intensification of human and social experiences. This intensification's medium is, more and more frequently, the image. Digital photos not only confirm existence, but also actively co-create new relations.

"Love" is the third chapter, and in it we focus on how new communication technologies such as mobile phones, Skype or photoblogs enter into intimate relationships. Media become intimate when the relationships they remediate are experienced as close and authentic. At the same time, web logic washes away clear divisions between the private and public. A new form of semi-public or private-public life emerges, where privacy can by made public through various means.By engaging the resources and functions of the public networks, onecreates an intimate, personal space online.

In "Technologies of Reflectivity" we focus on the role of new media as tools of communalization and individualization. By remediating the creation of new types of communities, media are also part of creating a unique form of the "self." In this chapter, we describe how new communication technologies become "technologies of the self" within identity-creation processes. An important part of this process is reflectivity – materializing fleeting thoughts, emotions and contacts in searchable databases, new media bolster self-development efforts which engage Web-sourced feedback.

Everyday life with new media is connected with a constant sharing of music, movies and links to interesting places online. In "Sharing", our fifth chapter, we show that through these actions communities of users create their online paths and communalize experiences and opinions related to the networked culture. From these processes of exchanging and sharing emerges a co-internet: a familiar, local, collectively built network. In this chapter we propose a model of cultural circulation which illustrates how identity-related practices of searching and sharing are, in effect, a multiplication –broadcasting and creating local audiences for cultural content.

In the sixth chapter – "Geeking out" – we show how new communication technologies enter into common practices of creating, learning and sharing enthusiasm, ability or knowledge – the various ways of "geeking out." When connected to the online world, energy, competencies and ideas no longer scatter but can actually become strengthened. Geeking out in the online era means participating in actions whose meaning and consequences can be much greater than the effort put in by each individual. Whether the geek out is collecting archival photos, learning everything about a favorite band or creating photo projects it can become more engrossing and develop faster when it becomes tied to the online world.

The seventh chapter deals with school. New media not only change old practices of school life, such as conversations in hallways and classes, doing homework or studying for a test together, sharing notes or cheating on an exam. The appearance of new media also poses new problems – most significantly, the reliability and validity of online knowledge in a school context. By encouraging group action in meeting (or eluding) school challenges and sharing resources and competencies – the architecture of new media becomes a challenge for an educational system based on evaluating individual effort. In this chapter, we question how school hierarchies and rules change when students and teachers become active online.

The material we've gathered poses new questions, especially ones dealing with how people retain agency in a world which appears as a digital database. Zygmunt Bauman writes that in a liquid modern world of new media, happenstance has replaced consequence, order has given way to chaos, and time appears to be torn into shreds, chopped into fragments with no past or future, filled with consequence-free episodes.

The final chapter – "New questions about cultural participation" – suggests that new-media related changes in the cultural environment demand a new vocabulary to discuss "cultural participation." Old categories, such as "consumer," become problematic, when people become involved in processes of co-creating cultural content and circulating it – often to the exclusion of cultural institutions.

How can we think about cultural participation, when the old categories have expired?

Foreword to English edition

This book is the result of an ethnographic study which looked at teenagers' everyday new media communications practices in Poland. Because of the methodology used, it is hard to claim it represents the entire population or identifies new trends. However, it should be considered as a keyhole view at the lives of several dozen young people and at a slice of a new, emergent, reality. The project was also conceived as bringing together various perspectives. This is why the project team was made up of young researchers representing various disciplines and experiences, as well as several research centers. We wanted to create a framework within which we could analyze this new media landscape using a broad spectrum of research perspectives. The report is augmented with commentary from experienced academics who approached the subject through varied perspectives.

One of the book's main focuses is the problem of cultural participation and the possible set of exclusions it generates. Differing notions of which practices constitute "cultural participation" and which do not, can lead to different categories of exclusion. This problem, both in Poland and beyond, features prominently in cultural studies debates and discussions regarding cultural policy. As we moves further and further away from normative definitions of participation, and as we become more cognizant of the decomposition of cultural canons, we embrace a vision of culture in which social processes play an increasingly key role. At the same time, we are faced with new challenges. Does the increased valuation of bottom-up creativity, which is an unequally distributed commodity, create new sets of barriers? Is cultural policy's recent embrace of these bottom-up media practices a way to enhance citizens' activities, or simply a way to legitimize Web 2.0 business discourse – and yet another way in which the state is retreating from intervention in the cultural sphere? Of course, the observations noted in this book do not provide final answers to these questions, but rather lead us to pose further ones.

By choosing to focus exclusively on young people, we consciously took the risk of producing a 'flattened' image. We are well aware that age (the key variable in Poland's digital gap phenomenon) does not explain everything. Especially since the processes of using media to customize cultural practices described in this report make the usage of common quantifiers questionable. Our project's starting point was the ethnographic method – used here also as a cultural studies tool. We believe that this insight into young people's everyday lives should be the basis for further discussions of issues such as cultural participation, its changing hierarchies and the role of technology. We believe that despite living in the age of Big Data, quantitative data – however important – sometimes does more to obscure reality than to reveal it. We are confronted with innumerable amounts of information, but to properly interpret it, we must be able to look at the world from the perspective of the individuals who generate it. After all, their perspective does not always coincide with ours. We want the descriptions and questions included in our book to help us understand the quantifiable data, but also to show that much of it does not reflect the changing reality, and that the tools used to gather it need adjusting.

Last but not least, we wanted this study to be considered as a part of public ethnography – for it to be relevant beyond the academic circles. In Poland, we achieved this goal. Our research project was widely commented on in the media, and even prompted action from government institutions. The report sparked a debate about the relevance of modern Polish schools' offerings to the students' lived experience. It also prompted new work on surveys and measurements of Poles' cultural participation b both the Ministry of Culture and National Heritage and the Central Statistical Office. Over the last two years, the report was referenced not only in sociology and media studies publications, but also in reports prepared for the Polish government. "Youth and Media" also provided the inspiration for further research projects exploring significant, but largely ignored, aspects of cultural practices described in it. One such project (Obiegi Kultury – Circulations of Culture) created a survey to estimate the informal circulation of media content in Poland. (The study's results are available at http://obiegikultury.centrumcyfrowe.pl/en). Circulations of Culture, published at the time of Europe-wide protests against ACTA (Anti-Counterfeiting Trade Agreement), launched a broad discussion over cultural policy and the "invisibility" of certain cultural processes from the governmental perspective. As I write, this debate continues.

Some of the credit for our project's public visibility should be attributed to its Polish-language website (http://www.wyborcza.pl/mlodziimedia). The site was an experiment in the presentation of research data – in addition to the report and a public comment mechanism, it featured Paulina Jędrzejewska's short film and Tomek Ratter's photographs. Ratter's photos were later part of the "The Summer of Youth" exhibition at Warsaw's Zachęta National Gallery of Art. The website's launch was accompanied by articles in the daily press (study co-author Mateusz Halawa wrote an article in Gazeta Wyborcza – Poland's largest quality daily newspaper) and professional publications (the cultural studies quarterly "Kultura Popularna" dedicated an issue to portions of the report and translations of texts which inspired its creation).

Clearly, the authors' expectations for the report's English-language version are not as ambitious. In the Polish context, "Youth and Media" was, in many ways, a ground-breaking effort. Globally, it is one of many similar projects. However, we want observations from Poland, and the evidence of the state of Polish reflection (or a part of it) on the subject of networked digital media's influence on cultural practices to be included in the global discussion of these issues. We want English-speaking readers to be able to compare similarities and differences in how new media functions and the state of the surrounding discourse in Poland and internationally. We also want to make good on a debt of gratitude toward authors beyond Poland, whose works inspired us to work on "Youth and Media," and some of whom graciously provided us with commentary on our project.

Mirosław Filiciak, October 2012

INTRODUCTION:
Remediation

The report we are presenting is the result of a research project in which we used ethnographic fieldwork and theories of culture, society and media in an attempt **to identify the basic dimensions of the social environment co-created by new media, and to describe the individuals growing up in this environment and the ways in which they shape it.**

New media

As this report will attempt to show, new media are not only technological artifacts, but also, a historically new type of thinking, experiencing and acting in society. Given this perspective, all discussions of 'new media' will always be a debate about tensions between the old and the new, and the forms of their co-existence. As Carolyn Marvin writes:

> New media, broadly understood to include the use of new communications technology for old or new purposes, new ways of using old technologies, and, in principle, all other possibilities for the exchange of social meaning, are always introduced into a pattern of tension created by the coexistence of old and new, which is far richer than any single medium that becomes a focus of interest because it is novel. New media embody the possibility that accustomed orders are in jeopardy, since communication is a peculiar kind of interaction that actively seeks variety. No matter how firmly custom or instrumentality may appear to organize and contain it, it carries the seeds of its own subversion. (1990:8)

In this manner, the term 'new media' refers to a broader social and cultural change, within which the appearance of new practices engaging new technologies has consequences beyond the direct ones. In this sense, this is not a report about new media, but rather, a report in which we follow problems, conflicts, or opportunities associated with new media in an attempt **to reconstruct broader cultural dimensions of life in a world remediated by digital media. The term 'remediation'** (Bolter, Grusin, 2000) **refers to the dialectical relationship between the old and the new forms of communications. This relationship is productive – people and objects-media engaged in it are creating new aesthetic forms, new types of communities and new types of subjectivity.** "... (W)hat is new about digital media lies in their particular strategies for remediating television, film, photography, and painting," write Jay David Bolter and Richard Grusin (2000: 50). We are looking at the way in which digital and networked media remediate not only older media, but also the practices which engage these media – and further the social environment co-created by these practices.

What is the meaning of "cultural participation" in a world remediated by digital media? To pose the right question about relations between people, institutions and cultural texts, we must understand the essence of ongoing remediations. Examples of remediations include the rise of communicators such as Gadu-Gadu (transl. note: chit-chat in Polish and a popular instant messaging client), systems for archiving and sharing opinions such as Nasza-klasa (transl. note: Our-class in Polish, a Polish social networking site), or cell phones, into personal relations which create an unprecedented intensification of togetherness. Remediation is also seen when behaviors surrounding learning and interactions with school meet a-hierarchical forms of non-sanctified knowledge such as Wikipedia, and *The Iliad* is not only a book in the school library, but also an mp3 file available online. Remediation also occurs when personal passions, such as creating, collecting or listening become more intense and productive when combined with online social networks of similar-minded people using the same practices.

All of these remediations do not run along plans and scenarios imposed in a top-down fashion. Nobody's remediating anything – with remediation, we are talking about emergent effects of social practices, for which the arrival of new digital forms of communication made a significant difference. Remediations – bundles of practices engaging the new media, are helping create networked and digital social contexts that are always local, whose results are always uncertain and the world emerging from them is unstable.

The problem with cultural participation (1)

These changes demand new ways of thinking about culture, and a new vocabulary to discuss it. We decided to pursue an ethnographic research model to attempt to identify processes which often escape our notice due to a lack of theoretical and research tools which would allow us to see them. Our fieldwork, with all of its inherent unpredictability and consciously open frames of reference, allowed our partners (the high school students in the field, our research team and the experts writing this report) to notice and identify these processes. In this report, Wojciech Burszta writes about "an inadequacy of most existing analytical terms (culture, free time, cultural activity, cultural identity, cultural canons, cultural participation)", (182) in the face of a changing social context. This observation is worthy of a pause, as it identifies one of the crucial problems of writing about and studying culture in times of remediation.

While writing this report, we often felt that many of these categories (most notably 'cultural participation') have become what the sociologist Ulrich Beck refers to as "zombie categories." (2002: 203) "Zombie categories" are the living dead of theory: they no longer refer to empirically describable events or significant social practices, but continue to haunt the discussion of them. Further, when used in empirical studies, they can create artifacts: results which despite the most scrupulous methodology and precise study do not describe the world which they supposedly depict. Our choice of ethnographic methods was meant to help minimize this danger. As Pierre Bourdieu wrote, ethnography is fieldwork conducted not only in the physical 'field' but also, simultaneously, in the philosophical sphere – the world of terms. (1990)

The difficulty of the ethnographic process involves the need to simultaneously utilize terms such as 'cultural participation' as research guidelines (as observation without a theoretical background misses the point), but also to modify, and even occasionally abandon these terms when they obscure the understanding or articulation of a problem. This is why this report uses the term 'cultural participation' sparingly, while, at the same time, it is a voice in the discussion of changes occurring in the field which is often described by this very phrase. We did not go into the field, to study if, and how, young people participate in culture. (One of the issues with "cultural participation" is that it is used both as a tool of exploration, but also to classify individuals as either participants or non-participants, as well as to impose normative distinctions between cultural and non-cultural events.).

We went into the field to observe social practices remediated by new media (while ethnographically participating in some of them), to consider whether it is productive to continue to think of culture as a separate, and usually institutionalized, sphere where individuals must be classified as either participants or non-participants. In our research, we found out that culture continues to escape from the influence of institutions, and that it is increasingly difficult to separate it from other spheres of our lives. **In the process of remediation, the question of "cultural participation" is less and less analytically and politically useful, while questions about forms of cooperation in the production of cultural texts, aesthetic, hermeneutic or social competencies associated with functioning among the flood of information, images and narratives, or the creation of conditions for the development of networked communities around cultural practices or cultural texts become ever more significant.**

In the report we used ethnographic tools to problematize everyday life in a world filled with new communication technologies, and to create a field for posing just such questions. The field experiences of ethnographers working on "Youth and Media," the discussions carried out for this project, and the directly relevant voices of Wojciech J. Burszta (181), Wiesław Godzic (178) and Marek Krajewski (185) convinced us that the search for a new language and categories of discussing culture, the relations between individuals and cultural texts and among individuals remediated by these texts is the most pressing matter.

Problematization

The matter of problematizing the evolving use of new media was a primary concern during the preparation, execution and writing of this report. We wanted to see what types of problems arise out of the social practices which the new media create. When referring to problematization – both as a process occurring in the world we are describing as well as our method of describing it for this report – we do not want to simply represent the world as we found it. (The report does not aspire to be an exhaustive description of the current "ways of the youth") We are also not interested in formulating "problems" which are removed from the practices we observed. (This is a limitation of the ethnographic method, as there are many potential topics which we do not discuss because our fieldwork and discussions did not lead us to consider them.) By problematization, we mean "the totality of discursive or non-discursive practices that introduces something into the play of true and false and constitutes it as an object for thought (whether in the form of moral reflection, scientific knowledge, political analysis, etc.)." (Foucault, 2001) One of the main work methods during this project was posing such problems and observing, how, in the context of social practices, do problems viewed as significant get addressed in people's everyday practices. In this report we pose problems based on social practices in which we co-participated, and which we attempted to theorize, while also observing how actors "in the field" posed problems (deemed something a topic of discussion or thought). In this sense, the ethnographic method of problematizing reduces the traditional distance between the observer and the observed, and between scientific and popular knowledge. For example, the issue of anonymity and privacy is not only a topic for journalists' inquiries about "Nasza-klasa" or academic articles about the sociological aspects of the internet. This problem comes into play in common social practices when our participant Marianna has to choose which of her Paris trip photos to post on Nasza-klasa and which not to, or when another participant is deciding whether to accept a new friend request. Similar issues arise around cultural participation or non-participation.

Rather than directly studying "cultural participation," this report looks at the problems which come into play when we focus on relationships between people and cultural texts or interpersonal relations remediated by these texts. If we agree that we are dealing with a process in which life's cultural dimensions are remediated, the problems which develop will be different and can be articulated using new categories. In this sense, the best answers to questions of cultural participation will be the answers to other, yet to be articulated questions or problem sets, which will come into play in a new, networked cultural environment. Among those discussed in this report, are:

- **Digitalization:** most cultural objects are stored as computer files, and are thus free from physical limitations – they are easily copied, moved and altered. For people who grew up surrounded by digital media, analog forms appear to be "flawed," they resist, they are not easily shared or circulated, this is why books, movies and other relicts of an analog past, while still utilized, are increasingly remediated and transformed into digital forms. The old media can still exist from an aesthetic point of view, but the logic behind today's cultural circulation is digital. In this report, we discuss the practices of sharing these texts, which are, in fact, multiplications of them, and the resulting overload of culture, which is increasingly difficult to characterize and sort.

- **Networked:** connected with the digitalization of cultural texts' circulation is the constant growth of commentary paratexts and metadata. In the internet era, culture is constantly on the move – it cannot be thought of as a static depository, a separate life sphere, as it is interlinked with other activities. Particularly significant is the fact that information networks retrace social networks (people scale the networks down using them mostly for reinforcement of face-to-face interactions). The internet allows the exchange of photos, music and films, but the reasons behind sending these files are variously motivated, with a high positive value placed on the desire to exchange, share, and gift links or files which reflect one's own passions, explorations and discoveries.
- **De-institutionalization:** institutions which traditionally determined cultural hierarchies and access to them are less and less significant as actors in the circulation of cultural texts. This freedom from institutional constraints which controlled access to culture has often led to a freedom from legal constraints as well. The digital networked culture is one of excess, most texts are stored on internet servers and hard drives belonging to friends and strangers, and the crucial problem is no longer access to culture but rather filtering it. These filters are often groups without institutionalized identities, with a status equal to that of their users. The divisions between professionals and amateurs, experts and consumers relying on the experts' knowledge are being redefined. Official canons are disappearing, hierarchies of goods are developed within groups connected by social interactions or shared interests. Connected to this phenomenon, is the rise of "closeness" and "authenticity" as the basic modalities of cultural-based togetherness.
- **(De)individualization and (de)linearization:** The technologies used by the youth we met during this project have a large potential for individualization: they allow personalization while providing access to a cultural database whose size allows nearly infinite individual choices. However, these technologies are also used to establish group identities and the making of shared choices which allow a scattered database to become a group-based narrative. This does not mean that these technologies are obstacles – they allow choices, letting subjects oscillate between the separate/individualized and group-based/shared. Two opposite social practices connected to audiovisual texts can serve as examples

of these trends. TV shows are frequently pulled out of the context of the broadcaster's schedule and downloaded from the internet, played on the computer – thus the theoretically linear TV show form is transformed into an element of the database of cultural texts, with decisions regarding it shifting from the broadcaster to the consumer. At the same time, YouTube videos which number in the millions, become 'televised' and through Gadu-Gadu links become part of the cultural landscape of groups of friends.

- **Openness:** in reference to Henry Jenkins' category of 'participatory culture' category (2006; see also p. 177 in this report), we should pay attention to culture's openness which, thanks to new media, lowers the barriers to artistic expression, while offering access to informal community practices and enhancing bonds between the participants. In this context, 'participation' is the result of users' activities and the capabilities offered to them by new technologies. Among them, Web 2.0 internet services in which various activities, including primarily communicative ones, are recorded and archived, effectively becoming creative in nature.
- **Reflectiveness:** Digital media's ability to record nearly all events remediated by technology enhances individuals' tendency to reflect on their actions. For example, the Last.fm service allows individuals to externalize and "see" their taste in music, reducing the previously nebulous category of taste into a material realm. Because of this, cultural texts which circulate (and leave multiple traces behind) and the choices associated with their consumption become visible to both the individual and their social surroundings. Thus creating critical elements in the establishing of a personal identity. In this sense, "culture," "lifestyle" and "atmosphere" emerge as problems of reflection and self-knowledge, as well as subjects of creative efforts.
- **Visuality:** the new media culture is a visual one, taking place on, and in front of, screens. Images – not just perceived, but also produced on a mass scale by 'plugged-in' individuals armed with cell phones and cameras – are becoming the primary tools of conveying meanings. While combining a photo's status as a cultural artifact with the deeply emotional social realm of shared exploration and experiencing the world.

The problem with cultural participation (2): Anka

Posing these problems in an area usually classified as "cultural participation," we are examining two meanings of 'cultural.' First, we are looking at culture as texts which are intentionally cultural in nature. It is with this meaning in mind that we usually pose questions about hierarchy (high/low), form (aesthetics), method of circulation, and institutions which create, spread and store culture. Second, we observe culture in the realm of everyday practices. In this, more anthropological approach, we usually pose questions regarding the purposing of experiences by individuals, the creation of a communal imagination and structures for experiencing, as well as the establishment of creative cultural identities and models.

These two approaches are obviously intertwined. In the process of forming identities, cultural texts play an important role, while at the same time these texts are products of a specific cultural environment. Much of the discussion surrounding cultural participation is closer to the first approach, posing questions such as which cultural texts are, and which are not, received by the public, while posing questions about what happens with these texts in an individual or collective identity contexts much less frequently. In choosing an ethnographic approach – both at the research level and in decisions about presenting our findings – we are trying to valuate questions connected with the forms of socialization and the mechanisms of identity creation and not, the sociology of using cultural institutions.

The change highlighted by the remediation process, touches upon both of these meanings of culture. The content changes because hierarchies are toppled, new aesthetic forms are developing, new methods of circulating are growing and the role of institutions is evolving. The practices of being together and existing individually are changing – as they are remediated by new types of technologies, which, as we will see, are becoming technologies of the self and co-create new types of subjectivity. The fact that remediation reaches both the problem sets associated with interest in culture as a collection of texts and institutions, as well as culture as historically specific cultural practices of being together and the self, further reinforces the primacy of finding new categories of understanding modernity. "Cultural participation," as postulated by individual participants in a culture seems inadequate as a category, as the process of social change accelerated by remediation is producing new individuals who create their identities differently, while culture, at the textual level, means something else as well.

For example, in carrying out the ethnography of a remediated world we met Anka, a 17 year old resident of Parna (all names of research sites and informants, as well as details that might identify them, have been changed to protect the anonymity of our collaborators) - a large city in central Poland.

Anka loves Werner Herzog's films. In itself, this is not that striking. However, her path to discovering the German director's oeuvre is rather surprising. It all started with music: Anka intensely listens to David Bowie. Reading up on the artist online, she noticed his so-called 'Berlin era,' a period when the artist lived in West Germany and recorded three albums inspired by local electronic music: *Low*, *Heroes*, and *Lodger*. Anka downloaded the three albums as mp3 files. Looking at her idol's sources of inspiration, she noticed the band Popol Vuh - a CD of which she borrowed from her uncle. It made a strong impression, and she began reading about the band online, where she learned that the German group recorded music for Herzog's films.

She is now a cinephile, but does not spend much time at movie theaters. (Besides, Parna does not host many Herzog festivals.) Instead, she is active in the discussion forums of a large movie portal, where she interacts with moviegoers who watch more and better films than her friends. It is these online acquaintances who suggest other Herzog films to her, and the names of several other directors, whose films she downloaded, watched on her computer screen and saved to her hard drive. Today, Herzog is her favorite filmmaker.

Anka's example illustrates the various processes now entangled with what is commonly known as "cultural participation." Regardless of the perspective we assume, the category would include her interactions with Herzog's movies, but, the manner in which Anka discovered his films, and how she watches them – less so. The model of cultural participation as a matter of practices turns out to be a mixture of various orders: the tips and suggestions for new movies is "crowd-sourced," the knowledge of anonymous or nickname-disguised forum members, who do not represent any cultural institution (unless the forum can be considered a 'cultural institution'). These are movie lovers who write about cinema, but they are not subject to any hierarchical verification. The knowledge and recommendations come from people like Anka, who are removed from hierarchical relations (where an individual with knowledge is above others), and from the teacher-student model (where the transmission of knowledge is built on a school-like basis, between an institution-teacher and receiver-student).

These people do not work at cultural institutions, cinemas or respected magazines (or, at least, Anka does not know if they do, as such an affiliation is not significant for her). Her interest in Herzog was also not a conscious choice of a "work of art," but rather the result of following the path of a music idol – a very simple practice for anyone moderately comfortable using the Web. The method of reaching the text is also far removed from traditional cultural patterns – the fact that Herzog's movies were not shown in any of Parna's cinemas was no obstacle for Anka, as she has unlimited access to cultural output thanks to the internet. (The movie subtitles are the work of anonymous internet users who share their work on a dedicated website, similar to the one attacked in 2005 by film distributor Gutek Film.)

Anka does not analyze whether what she is doing is legal. (Many of her cultural participation practices listed here, amount to crimes under Polish criminal law. Which is why we've changed her name and the name of the city in which this September 2009 narrative takes place. There is another reason for this anonymity, and this topic is much broader than Anka herself. There are tens of thousands such people in Poland -- this is how cultural participation looks in Poland.) Copyrights and the legality of copies do not come up as significant in discussions with Anka. The ease of access to digitized culture on the internet suspends discussions about ownership. As the father of one of Anka's friends said: "the young think that whatever is online is just theirs."

Let us go on. The 'screening' of a movie on a household computer challenges the typical order of matters: Anka is not sitting in a movie theatre, she's sitting in front of her internet-connected computer. With the press of a button, the window screening *Nosferatu* is blocked by the Gadu-Gadu window in which Anka is talking with her friend. After all, the computer plays many roles in her life, and "cultural participation" is just one of them.

How she stores her movies is also significant: her room lacks the hallmarks of a movie collector's den, there are no DVD or VHS box-sets of movies, but her hard drive holds hundreds of movies. Because of Herzog and other directors, Anka is learning Russian, because, as she says, Russian-language websites have a great selection of movies. After watching several of Herzog's films, she is no longer just a consumer of culture, she takes part in forum discussions, recommending movies to her online peers. She is affecting their cultural choices and the texts which they use.

In a remediated, digital world we are describing, cultural texts (such as Herzog's films) become computer files – circulating on the web to be downloaded and copied. Their audience is also different from the typical cinema crowd – it is a networked audience for whom an interest in Herzog's films is more important than their physical location (cinema) or time (showing). In this way, Herzog and his films gather people from all around Poland. This, however, is not reflected in the film distributors' statistics, or in studies on Polish youth's interest in cinema, or scientific terms which deem Anka as either a consumer of official, institutionalized culture or as a non-participant.

INTRODUCTION:
Connected and online, the ethnography of a digital world

If Your Kids Are Awake, They're Probably Online.
"The New York Times"

In this report we used the theoretical tools of contemporary anthropology, sociology and media studies, as well as ethnographic methods, to follow youths traveling on the human-technological networks, to find terms which would better capture the experiences of living in a remediated cultural environment.

A new existential situation

New media are fundamentally altering the way in which we experience the self in space and time.

This report illustrates what happens when atom-based physical space is overlaid with a byte-based web of transfers powered by cell phones, and increasingly, wireless internet. Being together with others becomes more intense when the physical realm is enhanced by mobile devices which allow a simultaneous connection to communication networks. Face to face contacts are enhanced by the attention paid to one another and exchanged online. Togetherness continues and can be experienced as being real, even when face to face contact ceases. Physical space gains new qualities, as long as network coverage exists, individuals comprising it enter into a unique "stand-by"/alert mode (see Marek Krajewski p. 54) which is related to the feeling of agency. However, it is also a type of a new semi-public life in which relations between closeness and privacy – intimacy and perceived privacy of the spaces in which this intimacy occurs are continuously subject to negotiations.

In a world remediated by digital technologies, the experience of the passage of time is connected with a feeling and expectation of immediacy and directness. What older generations may see as an acceleration (Gleick, 2000; Eriksen, 2001), appears to be the natural pace of the passage of time to the youths with whom we worked. However, ethnographic studies show that the way in which new technologies are altering the forms of experiencing the present, remembering the past and anticipating the future, is unique from a historical perspective. Technologies such as digital photography, web communicators or cell phones are altering the relationships between the past, present and future. In the era of immediacy, time may appear to be a pointillistic period of scattered instants (see Zygmunt Bauman, p. 169-171), and by mediating memory, media become a tool of a reflective manipulation of time. Digital photos shared online allow individuals to use images on an unprecedented scale, and also, to alter time by projecting future memories through the use of specific conventions in representing the 'present." (see p. 62) Paradoxically, the acceleration of experiencing and broadening of the present, at a loss to the past and future, creates specific nostalgic forms of both illustrating and experiential structures.

Time is not only changing its quality, but is also multiplying: tools such as mobile phones, high bandwidth connections and multitasking software makes it possible to do several things at the same time and transform reality in a multi-channel manner (some refer to this as cultural ADHD, a deficit of attention and others, its multiplication).

The transformations of time and space create new frames for the modern cultural environment. This re-organized space and time produces a new type of individual. Identity is shaped differently when being oneself and being with others is remediated by digital and networked media.

Melded to media, participating in culture

The young people whom we met while creating this report were just entering adulthood. They are the first generation which grew up with networked technologies. They do not remember an analog world. In the beginning of this report we describe an eighteenth birthday party this is both similar, and dissimilar to such events in the past. It is completely tied to the logic of digital media. The young are thoroughly melded with these media: laptops come to bed so that a Skype-accessed boyfriend can be close, exams are written with one mp3 player earbud in because its easier to focus on writing while listening. Cities are overrun by human-technological hybrids (youths melded with their mp3 players), who use music to govern their experiences, intensifying or muting their emotions or memories.

Our ethnographic studies notice warmth, intimacy and affect to this melding of individual and technology, that compels the use of biological or even organicist descriptions. In comparing social networks to the neurological system, Małgorzata Jacyno writes about tissue composed of mediated media relationships. (p. 87) The authors of this report cannot help help but be reminded of Mizuko Ito's (2008) metaphor of an ecosystem, while Marek Krajewski writes about media as a "type of second nature" (p. 30-32). What intuitions drive these formulations?

Second, **this surprising notional closeness of the affect and the algorithm, which bring in metaphors of melding, eco-systems and nature, challenge deep-**

seated cognitive patterns of separating the "human" and the "technological" into two fields, in which only the human holds the power of agency. If we show, as we attempt to do in this report, that memory, identity building, togetherness, creativity and learning are all subject to digital and networked remediation we must seriously consider the theories of Bruno Latour who attempts to create a new, non-anthropocentric anthropology (1993).

In order to properly pose the question of cultural participation, we must do so from within the center of modern cultural life remediated by modern media. This is a place where the processes of identity creation and the exchange of cultural texts enter into surprising relations, which do not allow us to think of "culture" as a separate field ruled by its own laws.

Asking about participation in culture today, we are also asking about the competency of using new media (media illiteracy), or perhaps about their physical forms. What technological-social status encourages or discourages a good and valuable life. This is why among the important new questions about participation in culture is the matter of online exclusion, which as we show in the report, (p. 104) is best thought of not as a situation affecting individuals but rather networks of people who either create or do not participate in a co-internet. These media-machines can be, as Marek Krajewski writes, "machines for creating bonds and relations." (p. 56) In this context, questions about participation in culture is a question about creating alliances which would allow the inclusion of culture in digital circulation.

Ethnography of new media

How to study this new environment?

The traditional goal of ethnography was observation: the model assumed a simple relationship between the "natives" and the "ethnographers." But, how to 'do' ethnography here, now and among yourself?

There was no dramatic divide between the youths and our ethnographers which would allow our work to focus on the traditional anthropological trope of difference, which is bolstered by physical distance. ("Imagine yourself suddenly set down surrounded by all your gear, alone on a tropical beach close to a native village, while the launch or dinghy which has brought you sails away out of sight," began Malinowski in *The Argonauts of the South Pacific*). Of course, our 'digital natives' are different than us – we remember a world without the internet – but we are still close to them: connected to the same networks and, to some extent, also melded to the media. More similar than different, we did not need a dinghy, as we are describing our own village. We have cellphones from the same operators, and some of us regularly update our Facebook profiles. The success of this project comes down to the incredible energy, imagination, inquisitiveness, sensitivity and intelligence of our ethnographers, as well as the much used – by both us and our partners – technologies: the invisible infrastructure of cell phones and emails, which connected people working in various parts of Poland, and the networked editing software, in which this report was composed. We ourselves our melded and connected.

Ethnography was traditionally descriptive. In the digital world things are not as simple: its residents continuously describe themselves, photograph themselves, and relate the details of their lives. Here, our ethnography challenges yet another ethnographic trope: representation. We do not claim to have a privileged point of view: our theory does not create a point of view which offers a better perspective, but rather, searches for knowledge which is located in the jungle of everyday life in the Gadu-Gadu, Nasza-klasa, photoblog and SMS era. We recognize that writing an ethnography of new media amounts to adding yet another representation to the stream of representations being produced – intentionally or not – in the practices engaging the media. We are describing – photographing, recording, quoting, copying and pasting, highlighting and linking a world which has been flooded by digital representations to a point where sometimes, the boundary between an event and its representation completely disappears (see p. 62). A world in which a glance leaves material evidence on social network profiles, where we do not only say "love you" but, also, love – simply by taking a photo (see p. 71).

This flood of representations does not fill us with a postmodern resignation. In this report we work hard to observe from the second-order (Niklas Luhmann), by studying everyday practices, techniques and styles of viewing, which are exemplified by our young collaborators. Describing the natural way in which they communicate using images is a challenge, but this specific remediation allows us to capture the process in which digital traces, left unwittingly on the web, as well as intentional presentations, become autonomous and gain the powers of agency. Our guides showed us a world in which digital photos and text archives have the ability to create new situations, motivate to act, and participate in identity processes.

Ethnography in a database

For all these reasons, our report is not a traditional ethnographic narrative based on the fantasy of a reconstructed cohesive whole. Such a form would be contrary to the spirit of the world which we saw during our research. The flood of digital (self)presentations, which help create this world, does not create too many 'cohesive wholes' and continuous narratives: we are trying to describe a cultural environment, whose time regimen is best described by Zygmunt Bauman as pointillistic (see p. 169-171). In it, the dominant cultural form is not the analog continuous narrative but rather a collection of rearrangeable elements. "Many new media objects don't tell stories; they don't have beginning or end; in fact, they don't have any development, thematically, formally or otherwise which would organize their elements into a sequence. Instead, they are collections of individual items, where every item has the same significance as any other. (Manovich, 2001: 218) We are describing a world which, to its residents, appears as a large database.

Of course, these theses about the fragmentation and disintegration of the world and the separation of experiences are not new – to some extent they have become the dominant self-description of modernity, to which many subscribe. However, ethnographic research allows us to go further and recognize the forces which are structurally contributing to this fragmentation (from individualization and change in social structures to the new forms embraced by culture), study the practices which allow this fragmented world to be carefully reassembled by these individuals. In the practices of searching, connecting or appropriating one can see emerging commonalities. When writing about the co-internet (p. 104) we show how the choices within the database are mostly group-based or seeking to create a group rather than individualized. The web is searched together and in the practices of search and scaling one can see a particular type of locality: the global database can be experienced as a close and familiar home environment. It is it that we are trying to reconstruct. In wanting to write an ethnography of a world which appears as a database, we are not searching for a whole where it does not exist – in the pluralism of narratives, the flood of information and the unsolvable contradictions of modern life.

The entirety which we are trying to grasp is contained in the practices of everyday life – the daily struggle to develop subjectivity. As Zygmunt Bauman, following Marx, writes in this report: people construct their subjectivity in an environment not entirely of their creation. That which we have at our disposal in a particular historical moment – the accessible construction material, the technical skills and procedures which are imaginable to us – affect how we are able to operate in the world, how we are ourselves and how we are with others. In this report we show that the materials from which we are building our subjectivity (cultural texts), and the technologies with which we accomplish it (techniques of self, see p. 87), change when digital and networked media come into play. Thus, we want to pose a question about the properties of these materials and technologies: "their virtues and faults, the capabilities they afford, and the limits which they impose." (Bauman, see p. 165)

How we worked?

For two weeks in 2009 – late august and early september – six ethnographers carried out observations and interviews with youths in three different sized cities.

Each ethnographer worked with a cooperator-guide of the same gender. We found these six critical people through social networks, the ethnographers' own networks, and, in one case, thanks to the recruiting network of the 4P research mix research firm. The six collaborators were paid for their work, the cooperation was guided by a contract, and when dealing with minors we also received their parents' permission.

In Zahaczewo, a town of 15,000 residents located some 50 kilometers from the regional capital, Michał Danielewicz worked with Filip, and Agnieszka Strzemińska worked with Kamila. (In the whole report we've changed the participants' names and details which would allow them to be identified online or offline, the names of their cities have also been altered).

In Parna, a city of nearly quarter million, Olka Gołdys worked with Gośka, and Jacek Szejda worked with Błażej. Before the recent administrative reorganization, Parna was the seat of a voivodeship.

In Ziemielin, the largest of the cities studied in our project, Paweł Mazurek and Paulina Jędrzejewska worked with Karol and Marianna, respectively. Ziemielin is a large city of over 600,000.

All of our collaborators, and most of their friends with whom we spoke, were high school students. Besides being the protagonists of this story, they also helped us reach other young people with whom we spoke, their girlfriends and boyfriends, friends, buddies and acquaintances. Thanks to this, we were able to gain a much broader and less fragmentary view of life with new media, but we also knew that we weren't talking with random individuals, but rather with people who had significant relationships with our collaborators. This way we combined the 'snowball' method – having spoken to 137 people – with a serious consideration for bonds, obligations and emotions connected to social networks, the impact of both strong and distant bonds.

The project team consisted of 10 people, the six above-mentioned ethnographers were joined by Mirosław Filiciak – the team leader, Agata Nowotny and Mateusz Halawa and the photographer Tomek Ratter.

Before the researchers went into the field, the team developed a research toolbox through a series of seminars and workshops which created interview scripts, photography guidelines and observation charts/tables. A constant part of fieldwork was the maintenance of study diaries and frequent phone consultations with the 'base.' These tools were meant to ensure that the process framework was fluid and elastic – as befits an ethnographic project. However, the observations and ideas found in this report were not the product of our research tools, but rather the attention to detail, imagination and sensitivity of the ethnographers who worked on this project. The most challenging aspect of their work involved describing ethnographically the youths' 'togetherness' – hanging around, looking around, talking, laughing, dancing, posing for photos, and wandering around town. We are also basing our findings on unstructured extended interviews, assisted computer and cell phone sessions, interactions remediated by cell phones, Gadu-Gadu, and Nasza-klasa, improvised focus groups and dyads, family interviews, virtual ethnography (thanks to which we were able to observe the electronic trails left by individuals in the internet, but also could remain in contact with our collaborators). Also, we carried out an experiment in which participants described their experiences of disconnectedness and connectedness (they agreed to refrain from using new media for a day, thanks to which they could see what they are missing out on, and break out of the complete obviousness of the new media which surround them). Additional tools used in this project were Tomek Ratter's photo project and Paulina Jędrzejewska's film.

In each town, our collaborators could shoot a short film. The researches had cameras, which they lent out to the youth and which were used according to their intuition. The resulting videos were edited and processed by Paulina Jędrzejewska. The team responsible for coordinating the entire project: Filiciak, Nowotny and Halawa – along with Tomek Ratter, also visited each of the three locations during the study. This allowed a better exchange of observations and experiences from each location, and also allowed the authors to become ethnographically engaged with the places they are describing.

A specific type of such engagement is Tomek Ratter's photo project which can be seen on p. 193 of this report. Entering our collaborators' world, Tomek proposed what he calls a "multi-faceted game with a camera." Taking photos, looking at the lens or not, finding cool places and changing uncool ones into cool by the use of an "aesthetic view," capturing and staging situations – all of these practices which are common for youths wondering around town with cameras became the subjects of conversations – all thanks to Tomek's presence. The effect is not a visual representation of this report but rather a photographic essay, an attempt to reflect, which uses photos as both its medium and its focus.

This study was developed during a series of seminars and workshops which featured guests like Tomasz Jędrkiewicz and Robert Zydel from

NUQ Research and Piotr Toczyski from Agora SA's research department.

During the seminars, we discussed the "Living and learning with New Media" report prepared by Mizuko Ito and her team in 2008. This three year, U.S.-based research project was financed by the MacArthur Foundation. Both Ito's research premises and her results were sources of inspiration for our research. Much like Ito and others, we are basing upon ethnographically described, material and life-based everyday social practices in which the youth are engaged with new media. Our approach to "working with youth," in which we decided to treat our collaborators as partners (co-workers) also owes a lot to Ito. In many social studies, youth are treated very "protectively" as individuals who are "not ready," "not yet fully developed" which often results in questions such as "what will become of them when they grow up," rather than question about who they are and how they act right now. Following Ito and the approaches of contemporary sociology of education, we recognized our collaborators as partners, who have their own lives, needs and desires. Even though they strongly depend on their parents and schools, and lack the full range of legal rights due their minority – they should be treated as partners (Ito, and others, 2008).

The other crucial text during our theoretical seminars was Nick Couldry's "Theorising media as practice," (2004) where he outlines a new perspective on media theory, which is much indebted to the sociological theory of practices. Couldry leaves behind the traditional media theory approach which treats media as either texts (posing questions of interpretation) or structures of production (posing questions of influences) and suggest understanding 'media' as social practices. Couldry's text was an important common structure for the interaction of researches working within media theory and scientists using more sociological tools and categories. Following Couldry, we posed our research question rather broadly: what do people do in relation to media, and what do people say in relation to media? Starting from such broad questions, we were able to discuss and develop our research project not to ask a narrow question of "computer use" but, we hope, one that allows us to capture large-scale cultural changes. The use of 'media' as a collection of broad and open sets of practices allowed us to give our ethnographers a large dose of freedom in pursuing how their collaborators moved around in a world filled with media. We wanted to allow ourselves to be surprised by this world.

This report is written by a five person team, based on six reports created by Michał Danielewicz, Olka Gołdys, Paulina Jędrzejwska, Paweł Mazurek, Agnieszka Strzemińska and Jacek Szejda. An additional source of information are three "exploratory" workshops following the fieldwork, and ongoing team consultations.

In this report we combine a research report and a scientific essay with ethnography understood as a manner of writing which focuses attention on details, evokes situations and remains closer to describing the atmosphere and particularity of the described world, than would be feasible in a more traditional analysis.

How to read this report?

The **main text** is organized in chapters which refer to the most important aspects of the everyday lives of the youths whom we studied: "Being together," "Love," "Interests/Passions," and "School," as well as chapters which focus on analytical categories significant to understanding the cultural environment created by the new media – "Intensity," "Technologies of reflection," and "Sharing."

Accompanying the main text are **highlighted parallel texts (such as this one)** which deepen our understanding of selected topics (for example: a suggested set of key phrases, p. 104), telling stories which allow a better feel for the world we are describing (going to an eighteenth birthday party, p. 42), or to understand the youth we are describing in the context of new media usage (for example, Karol, who uses the web for political activism, p. 83). Sometimes these sidebars act as a magnifying glass, allowing us to study one case and understand it in the larger context of the chapter. Sometimes, they are independent excursions, which begin with the questions posed in the chapters, but explore them with other aspects.

We've also highlighted **expert opinions** which correspond to the practices we are describing. These were requested at the project's start, but were consulted and prepared following the ethnographic fieldwork and during the writing of this report. These opinions sometimes take the form of an interview (for ex. Miroslawa Marody's text on p. 93), sometimes as commentary (ex. Josè van Dijck – p. 62), and occasionally an autonomous essay (ex. Marek Krajewski – p. 54). The placement of expert opinions in the text was entirely our editorial decision.

The entire structure is intended for linear reading, but, we can imagine that readers of the main text can choose to bypass one of the parallel texts to return to them eventually.

BEING TOGETHER

We are on the Island in Ziemielin. A dozen of us are sitting on the concrete-lined waterfront – around us other similar groups. It's dark; the illuminated facades of old buildings are reflected in the water. Young people are sitting on the lawn, on benches; chatter and laughter surround us. Our group is drinking beer, occasionally they reach into a bag where vodka and juice are hidden. The vodka is poured into photo film containers which function as makeshift shot glasses. Marianna, Agata, Alek, Krzysiek and *Młody* are with us. They joke around and hug a lot. There will be cool photos from today – smiling, hugging, making faces. They look straight at the camera. End of the summer.

We are at a campfire in Zahaczewo with our guide Kamila. The party is on the outskirts of the city, in a spot between two small valleys. You can not get here by an accident – the complicated route goes over a hill, a field and a path through the forest. Danek organized it. People in the know say he put the party together, hoping that Magda would come. Unfortunately, to Danek's disappointment, Magda went with her, as people say, *new almost boyfriend*, to a different campfire. The event was carefully prepared, yesterday some of the guys brought wood, chopped it and set it aside, leaving a few stumps so that those without blankets could sit down. People are coming and going – friends and acquaintances talk about this party as well as another one, one valley over. That campfire is organized by other local youths, who due to their fondness for cheap liquor, are referred to as "Sulfurites" (transl. note: sulfur refers to the burning sensation of poor quality wine). Even though the last few weeks have been full of parties, Kamila and her friends know this evening is somehow special. Somebody jokes that everybody dressed in dark colors, kind of like at a similar party last year, when they used to meet up more frequently and listened to 'harder' music. Nostalgia's in the air – it's not only the end of summer, but there's also the unsaid thought that in a year many of them will move to large cities and there won't be parties like this anymore.

Parna, Friday around 5 p.m. Błażej and his buddies are thinking about what to do tonight. Wojtek suggests going to "Atut," a club in the city center. The guys think of it as a special place – to get inside you have to know the code to the intercom, only then do the doors open. They are clearly proud they know the code, and when asked how they know it, they exchange sly laughs and say *you just gotta know these kinds of things*. The club is filled with cigarette smoke, there are books on the shelves – decoration. Eventually the guys settle in – we are sitting together, drinking beer and talking. Błażej, Łysy, Marcin, Łukasz and Bartek. Marcin wants to hook up with Monika, a good looking chick. The guys have tons of advice – Marcin is shy, he's not taking advantage of all his opportunities. It's about 10 p.m. when Łukasz suggests a change of venue. We leave.

In this report, we show how being oneself and being together are now constantly remediated by media. The connected and online youth with whom we worked on this ethnography of a digital world are celebrating the end of the summer at parties, which remind us of those we knew from an analog world. Looking more closely, however, we can see that everyday life practices are transformed and boosted by new networked technologies. Initially easily overlooked, new media co-create the space in which our young collaborators meet, remediate their relations and help them understand themselves.

However, we consciously began our story on an island, at a campfire, and at a club. This is where events important to our young collaborators take place. We could have begun in a sensationalist tone, showing a young man with bags under his eyes, spending another night playing a computer game or a girl sending text messages in class. But, after spending two weeks with these youths, we can see that the most important things are friendships, first love, cuddling and holding hands. The proximity of sharing a beer, or talking while smoking cigarettes. Being together is most important – nothing will replace face to face interactions and looking each other in the eye. Still, not everything is as it was, new media co-create the space in which our young collaborators meet, remediate their relations and help them understand themselves.

Ziemielin. Krzysiek drinks another shot of vodka. Unlike the others, his day began at school. He was retaking a physics exam in the morning. At 7:30 a.m. Marianna sent him a text message: "*battle time!*" His reply was "*check optical mirror for me quick.*" The message is economical. There's no place for *thank yous* or *pleases* – every second counts. The answers to questions on optics could mean a lot for him. Marianna, still groggy, immediately turns her computer on, getting angry that it's so slow – *that piece of junk!* She opens a browser – too hastily – the system freezes up. She gets even angrier. She's stressed because Krzysiek is waiting for her help. (At the same time our ethnographer Paulina Jędrzejewska notices Marianna went online from her computer across town – she's available on Gadu-Gadu. Paulina asks her to meet up later on, but gets no response). Marianna's fighting with the internet, her stress level is rising. She clicks on the Internet Explorer icon at least a dozen times and ...nothing. Finally, the window opens. And then, a million others – one for each nervous click. The mirror is on *Wikipedia*, Marianna sends the text, it's almost eight, and that is when Krzysiek's exam starts.

Krzysiek passed, there's reason for celebratory drinks. (Later on, he'll tell Marianna that he didn't understand anything from her text.)

By the campfire in Zahaczewo, music blares from small speakers connected to a phone, or rather, several phones. There's an argument anytime someone wants to plug in their phone to play their songs. The songs are downloaded mp3s, burned onto CDs, transferred to portable memory cards. Nobody brought their computer to the party, but a part of their computers' contents is always with them. Before leaving home, phones get connected to computers and music is transferred. They walk around town with several gigabytes in their pockets.

The internet, computer, cable, cell phone, a party to go to.

Its getting darker. The phones glow in the dusk. Our Zahaczewo guide Kamila, is constantly answering her phone, checking text messages. It's her boyfriend Bartek, who's not here (but he clearly is). Bartek doesn't really know this crowd, and besides, he'd rather avoid Kamila's ex who's also here. Bartek makes up for his physical absence through constant phone contact with Kamila – the whole time he knows exactly how the party's going. He'll know further details in a couple of hours when Gadu-Gadu statuses change, and the first photos will appear on Nasza-klasa profiles and blogs, quickly joined by a flood of comments.

Back from a party, camera, cable, computer, internet.

Friday, almost 5 p.m. in Parna. Błażej takes a look at his phone. Usually around this time, a friend calls, the text messages start coming in. Plans need to be figured out, where to go, what to do. Finally, a text message from *Łysy*: 7 p.m. at "Atut" club. Błażej leaves home, we meet up in front of the club and go in. The guys are talking about Monika – Marcin likes her. His friends ask if he hit her up on Nasza-klasa or chatted with her on Gadu-Gadu. He really ought to try. Time flies, there's an idea to change places. The guys simultaneously take out their phones. Today's not going to be too wild, but its worth checking to see what other people are doing, what's going on. They do not want to find out tomorrow that they missed out on something big.

The invisible media co-create communication platforms which allow these everyday social togetherness practices to occur. The media accompanied the participants throughout the parties. They also ensure, that the evenings described here will remain with them for a long time as photos and comments – material version of memories of time spent together. The media's invisibility at The Island, the campfire or the club is not the result of its absence, but the opposite – the almost complete melding of the youths' social practices with them.

The young people reached the locations of the parties thanks to descriptions on Gadu-Gadu, where their friends posted information about the gatherings, and to brief conversations (cellphone minutes are not free) and text messages traded by friends and acquaintances. These people are important to them, and that means they remain in constant contact. Without new media the people in these descriptions wouldn't get to the parties not only because they wouldn't know where they are taking place. Also, because without the numerous means of contact offered by new media, they wouldn't be as important to each.

However, media are not only allow the young people to get to the parties, they create a communication platform where these various social practices can take place. They do not disappear when non-computer and non-phone contact is possible, when you can touch each other and share a common space. The media are still there, in their pockets, backpacks, on park benches or sidewalks. Only their role changes. They adapt to situations: telephones provide entertainment thru music downloaded from the internet. If the party is fun, they are also used to get others to come, if it's not going well, the media can be used to find others to join in. Phones and specially brought cameras let them capture the events, Jameson's "nostalgia for the present" (see Appadurai, 1996) is not unknown to these beer-drinking high schoolers. But, it's not only about that – a photo shoot can also be a lot of fun in itself. And when somebody has to step aside for a minute, their phone became a handy flashlight.

The media will also be involved in these parties in the days to follow – when the participants will be home, cleaning their rooms, eating meals with their parents and getting used to the idea that early mornings will soon return to their lives. Their Nasza-klasa profiles, photoblogs and Digart will have photos to show how fun it was to be together. And even if Alek will not see Marianna, Danek will not see Kamil's face, and Błażej will not see his friends, they will all know from their rooms that their friends are also looking at the photos and smiling, reminiscing about the night. They may also listen to songs they liked at the party thanks to links sent along by last night's 'DJs' who are proud that their selections were appreciated. All of these media traces of the end of summer parties – available on the web, but inaccessible or not understandable to strangers – will exist as new parts of the participants' friendships.

At the 18th birthday party

Sunday was the most important day of Marianna's last week of summer vacation. It was then that she was organizing an eighteenth birthday party along with Karolina – a classmate. *At a very cozy chillout cafe "Cisza."* Marianna's been to "Cisza" a number of times, it's one of her favorite places. First, she likes the atmosphere (the music, people, and the austere but warm interior with retro elements). Second, she's never been asked for an ID there. Until last Sunday, that was a very important consideration. Marianna treats alcohol as an optional addition to a club party, but she wants her not drinking to be an independent choice, not the result of some imposed ban.

Those more fortunate often feel bad for friends with July and August birthdays, whose parties are often marked by absences. Instead of personally wishing Happy Birthday at house parties, many friends send text messages with greetings from the Mazurian Lakes. However, end of August turned out to be pretty fortunate for Marianna. Most of her friends were back in town, her friend Iza got back from a family trip to the seashore. A week earlier, Marianna finished her summer job which took up most of her vacation. (For two months, five times a week, she waited tables from 11 a.m. to midnight at an elegant restaurant on the market square, saving money for her own laptop, as she currently shares a computer with her brother.) School hasn't started yet, and she was able to get the 50 percent discounted summer rate to rent out the bar for the night.

All the best on your birthday!!!!!!!

Creating the mp3 playlist is an extended process. The stakes are high, as music plays a large part in whether people will have fun. In choosing the music, Marianna was strongly influenced by her friend Iza's experiences with her eighteenth several months ago. It was those mp3 which filled the memory stick. Good old rock n' roll, dance friendly pop-hits and a bit of disco polo (transl. note: Polish, folk-inspired dance music targeted at mostly rural audiences) *just for laughs.*

The rest of the tunes were CDs with songs selected by Marianna, and downloaded and burned by her boyfriend Jurek. Marianna doesn't have high speed internet, and, besides, she often relies on Jurek for computer help. He usually installs and configures new software for her. The music was played from his laptop.

Our ethnographer Paulina Jędrzejewska spent Sunday morning at the supermarket with both girls. It was supposed to be a quick trip for chips, snacks, balloons and streamers. Marianna was saying that people do not really eat at clubs, but her Mom eventually convinced her that *you have to offer something to your guests*. The shopping list grew. (In the afternoon, when her aunt will be giving Marianna her birthday make-up makeover, Jurek, Karolina and a cousin will be busy making sandwiches.) At the store, the list expanded thanks to spontaneous ideas (*A dip for the carrots! – How do you make it?! – I'll call Gośka, she made it for her party...*). Everybody buys alcohol at the bar which is hosting the private party – that's how it makes money. (Of course, you occasionally go around the corner with three friends and a bottle of cherry vodka.)

Two hours before the party, Marianna and Karolina's closest friends decorate the bar. The cheap supermarket streamers straightened out before the party even started. Over 80 people came to "Cisza." Marianna sent most invitations through Nasza-klasa – the simplest way with a database of almost all her friends. Some people, not on Nasza-klasa, were invited by Gadu-Gadu or phone. The girls invited their entire class, along with some 30 additional people each. Marianna's 30 consists of her closest friends (except for Jurek with whom she spends most of her free time), a couple friends from middle school, family (mom, brother, cousin, two aunts, an uncle) and Jurek's friends.

Through Nasza-klasa Marianna invited her long unseen teacher from middle school. This is how she found out he no longer lives in Ziemielin: *i'm teaching by the sea now near the town where i was born and raised, best wishes – all the best on your birthday!!!!!!!!!!*, he wrote on Nasza-klasa.

A hanger for the fashion blogger

The girls decided to not spend money on a professional DJ. They set the playlist, and the tracks changed whenever somebody came up with a new idea. In the end, Marianna's closest friends dominated the DJ booth, taking some requests from the floor. The tables at the bar reflected relationships with Marianna: middle school friends together, closest friends together and the family together. Things went similarly with the shared presents.

Only Iza bought an individual present for Marianna. It was a symbol-gift – a coat hanger with a raspberry shawl tied around it – which was related to Marianna's recent desire to become a fashion blogger/stylist (see Aestheticizing, p. 78). Marianna will confirm the gift's artsiness by hanging it on a wall in her room. A fashion blogger/stylist is a person who has their own photoblog dealing with fashion. The blog features one's own photos in personally styled outfits with comments. A blog entry is usually similar in form to a fashion shoot in a lifestyle magazine: a brief description of the clothing along with information on where it was bought, the price, and a general characterization of the whole outfit). In general, these descriptions are longer and more personal than those in magazines.

The party photographer is Jurek's friend, who has an almost-professional digital SLR camera which works well in the dark interior thanks to an internal flash. Among Marianna's closest friends there are those interested in photography, but they mostly stay away from photographing events and, besides, they came to have fun and party and not to create art.

Most of the photos from the party will be posted on a middle school server operated by Marianna's friends. The first year we paid fifty zloty out of our own cash, but then we asked the principal who agreed to pay for it in the future. When we graduated from middle school we wanted to encourage younger students to keep the forum up. We even recorded and uploaded a YouTube a movie about a relay race where we're running around a parking lot in suits – totally embarrassing. But that was the time Nasza-klasa got popular, and nobody wanted to keep up the forum and all conversations moved onto Nasza-klasa and the forum died away – explains Marianna's friend Krzysiek. There's still a regularly paid for server mostly used by the forum veterans – middle school alums, who use it as a shared hard-drive to store and share photos with friends (the school seemingly forgot that it pays for it, and isn't aware of its new use). The best photos will show up in Nasza-klasa galleries posted by Marianna, Karolina or their boyfriends.

18 lashes

So-so party, dance floor empty, Hania sends a text message to a friend around 10 p.m. With time, however, more and more people get up from the tables, the cherry vodka drinkers come back inside. People dance on the concrete floor: alone or in pairs, in a circle, in a crowd, rhythmically bobbing around and creating involved comical dance arrangements. The best received songs are the best-known ones, ranging from *Baranek* by Kult to the discopolo hit *Niech żyje wolność* (Long live freedom) by the band Boys. People not only dance but also sing along: "*Na głowie kwietny ma wiaaaaanek*" (she's got a flower gaaaarland on her head...).

The evening's high point comes at midnight: "Happy Birthday" sung by all, a birthday cake with sparkling candles and the ceremonial dubbing as an adult. Marianna peacefully accepts the 18 belt lashes on her buttocks. The hits vary, from the mercifully light taps to fairly serious smacks.

The crowd stays on the dance floor until 4 a.m. The next day – her first as a full-fledged adult – Marianna and Jurek wake up at 5 p.m.

To our young collaborators, face to face interactions remain the fullest and most valuable form of contact. It is worth underlining this, as our subjects frequently stated some hesitations toward screen to screen interactions, which stemmed from the limits of these communication forms, and, at times, even a degree of distrust toward them (especially when concerning meeting new people). it is also worth mentioning this as many parents, teachers and journalists fear that new media has become a replacement for direct interactions, that young people "sit at home in front of the computer instead of spending time outside." The belief that the online and offline worlds are separate is a persistent hold-over from the early 1990s, when the internet actively entered our apartments and offices as a promise of a new modernity. As described by Canadian sociologist Barry Wellman, it was a "technological miracle." This miracle was supposed to erase previous tenets of social interaction, an idea reinforced by academic and journalistic descriptions of virtual worlds where the cyber-pioneers experimented with their identities, created friendships with unseen individuals across the world, abandoned the limitations imposed by their physical selves to pursue their fantasies and suffered at the hands of invisible and unknown persecutors who lingered in the back alleys of the online world. Scientists finally found these new, nearly virgin, Trobriand Islands located only a few mouse clicks away.

> "Some pundits went too far, extrapolating from (...) esoteric online settings to the generalized Internet experience. However, as the Internet became broadly adopted, it became clear that communication would not primarily be with far-flung mysterious others in virtual worlds, but with the people whom users already cared about most:

family, friends and workmates. Nevertheless, ideologies of the unique, transformative nature of the Internet persisted (...) long distance community ties had been flourishing for generations, using automobiles, telephones, and airplanes."

(Wellman, Hogan 2004: 1)

In the world in which we participated during this project, Gadu-Gadu, Last.fm and Nasza-klasa are mostly used to communicate with people who are seen everyday: at school, the neighborhood, parties or concerts. In some instances these are friends, sometimes acquaintances, but actual strangers appear very infrequently. A conversation with a stranger is as rare of an occurrence as it was before the internet era – they happen occasionally, but are the exceptions rather than the rule. Especially because a face to face friendship, in contacts remediated by the internet, limits the opportunity for misunderstandings. Brief, almost short-hand texts, even when enhanced or mellowed by emoticons, require a familiarity with the conventions, the sender's personality and a trust in their intentions in order for them to be fluid and clear. As Marianna told our ethnographer: *I only talk on Gadu-Gadu with people I know, because I can see their faces*. Błażej from Parna said: *All of these verbal and non-verbal gestures which happen when we see each other, that's the essence of our interactions, our conversations. On Gadu-Gadu all of that is reduced to nothing.*

The power of close bonds

Regardless of the internet's potential as a global technology which allows maintenance of weak bonds more effectively than ever before – our collaborators' internet is clearly mostly a way to keep up bonds with a group of closest friends. Of course, services such as Nasza-klasa can be described as a bolstering of weak bonds – among our high school-aged collaborators there was a consensus that a 'friend' can be anybody you say *Hi* to. Thanks to the portal, the network of relationships which would have atrophied without the internet grew, and, just as significantly, became more reflexive. However, that's a question of Nasza-klasa's unique properties, which, unlike more specialized social networks (the photo and graphic-based Digart which we discuss later and Last.fm), is viewed as an address book and functions as an online institution which is almost required to function in the community. This is where pre-exam notes are posted, along with party invitations and everything else. Nasza-klasa's broad reach means that contacts on it are not viewed as particularly significant: being one of several hundred friends does not compel activity or help for the other. It is useful as a tool for total mobilization, for example, if you are organizing a fundraiser for a cause, or want to buy or sell something, the contact list allows a broad reach for the *de facto* classified ad. **However, most time is spent interacting and strengthening relationships with a group of closest friends. Thus, it is not surprising that the new media-aided social practices we observed reflect this fact.**

One of our report's thesis is the argument that new media enhance and intensify the experience of being together. This intensification takes many forms. One of the first observations made by our ethnographers was the frequent use of new media to coordinate face to face meetings. This will be the starting point of the report's next part.

If we wanna play football, we usually look who's available on GG (transl. note: Gadu-Gadu). We start a group chat asking if we're playing, it's, more or less, a stable group of 10 people, and people say they're in. If we're still short, we send a private message to people outside the group chat. If we still don't have enough, then a phone call 'Are you playing?' goes out. I usually send a text messages but here I need to know the answer right away. This is how the guys in Zahaczewo put a football match together.

Black boxes, or material culture in the new media era

What creates generational differences these days, are not only media-objects, but also how different generations use them in the process of creating communities. **Marek Krajewski**, a sociologist at Poznań's Adam Mickiewicz University corresponds with **Agata Nowotny**.

Agata Nowotny: Focusing on the new media and youth practices associated with them, our attention frequently turned to the immaterial – the digital world flowing through the networks of data and algorithms which co-create social relations. But, there is a world of bytes and a world of atoms. We are wondering what makes up the material culture of our modern digital era. The materiality and agency of things is still important: our ethnography shows that the "internet" or "music" are bundles of practices, entangled with objects. Batteries, bundles of cables, monitors, earphones, keyboards, scratched cellphone cases... New media are often talked about in a fashion which suggests a fluid transfer of data and the elimination of geographical limits, space and materiality losing out to virtuality. Thinking of materiality in a digital era, we want to pay attention to the everyday practices connected to media, which are related to close contact with objects and through dealing with objects.

Media-objects have their own lives and circadian rhythms. It's Friday afternoon and Błażej, our 17 year old collaborator, knows that his cellphone is about to ring. This requires a set of appropriate actions – making sure its laying close-by, is charged and ready to be picked up. His and his friends' Friday night would not go as planned without the coordination allowed by it.

Karol is wondering around with his clique in Ziemielin. Everybody's got a cellphone but it is his that rings most often. Why? Karol looks the oldest, his phone gives his younger-looking friends access to beer, as they wouldn't fool anyone at the liquor store. On Friday night he gets a text message *buy us beer*.

Gośka's computer is turned off in the mornings. *Why would I turn it on* – she says – *if nothing's going on there at that time?* 'There' meaning inside an internet-connected computer – and more specifically – in the social network supported by Gadu-Gadu and Nasza-klasa. When Gośka is at school, her computer is asleep. It returns to life only after she gets back, when her friends sit down to their computers as well. In front of the computer, with the computer and sometimes on the computer she does her homework. There are at least three of here friends 'there' on Gadu-Gadu and she can be with them for at least three hours. Her computer desk also sometimes functions as a vanity table.

Another important object for her is her iPod. She's very proud of it; she wanted it for a long time. This is why she keeps it in a special woolen case to protect it from scratching and breaking. The experience of an iPod is not merely a musical one, it also involves caring for an important object, which is significant not only for its function but also in itself.

Each evening Kamila goes to bed with her mp4 player. (I'm also writing these words in bed with a laptop on my knees. We take these plastic objects with us to bed, not being conscious of how it affects our and their functioning. They stop being merely functional objects, we enter into relationships with them. Sometimes very intimate ones – we sleep with them, get angry at them and talk to them. They can get on our nerves: *my computer's very slow, I can't stand not doing anything on it*, they can calm us down and help us fall asleep).

Music brings Kamila to sleep. Her earphones play for twenty minutes, later, when she gets a bit sleepy, she turns the player off so that the battery won't run down.

They both go to sleep.

Marek Krajewski: Using Bruno Latour's distinction between mediators and intermediaries (Latour 2005; Abriszewski 2008: 269), we can say that the devices connected to telecommunication, radio, television and internet networks used by youth belong to the latter, not former category. This means, that they are a non-problematic and transparent element of their world, the relation system, which constitutes it. The significance of these devices and their role is negotiated, analyzed, becomes controversial and generates conflicts for parents, teachers and those who attempt to find an answer as to how did these communities come to exist, where people and media have become so inexorably melded.

In asking about the materiality of telecommunication media, which form an integral element of the youth ecosystem, I mostly see a sociological problem rather than a social one. Therefore, I assume the perspective imposed on us by the status of telecommunication media in the youth culture, in their everyday practices, and ask what is its essence, how does it fulfill itself. On the other hand, I am not attempting to problematize this status, by highlighting its negative consequences, using the lives of the youth's parents or grandparents as points of reference. I am also not asking whether it is good or bad that digital media is such an obvious and natural aspect of the youth's world.

Assuming such a perspective, allows us to notice that **what generates the inter-generational gap, is not the object itself, the possession of it or even its use, but rather, the form in which it is incorporated in the process of creating a community**. This is why we are faced today with the universality of ownership and utilization of communication media, but with significant differences in the roles that they play in socialization. It is this difference that generates the physical and instinctive differences between different social categories, a difference, which exhibits itself both in types of actions, and in experiencing and thinking. This difference is not based on world-views (but it can manifest itself in attitudes), ideologies (but can show itself in different ideas about life and the world), or axiology (but can create varying value systems), but rather on a somatic-technological one, forced upon us by the differences in how different generations view their bodies in a new technological environment. Barbara Fatyga once wrote about the separateness of the symbolic universes of different generations, differences which not only precluded understanding between members of separate ones, but also precluded research on subjects from different generations (see Fatyga 2001). While agreeing with the general thesis of generally separate worlds inhabited by each generation, it is worth noticing that today this division is a consequence of the **participation in different communities made up of people and objects**.

For example, we all use cell phones, using their functions, but our relations with them are significantly different, **creating intergenerational divisions which are not rooted in world view, but rather in differences in relations between objects-media and our bodies**. The division between old and young is also not rooted at the level of competencies in using these telecommunication objects – if we were to assume so – it would mean that programmers, IT specialists and electronics salespeople were eternally young. Also, it would ignore the fact that young people are often incapable of using those capabilities of these devices which are not necessary to their everyday lives. (For example, database searching, navigating the e-bureaucracy, creating properly edited documents.) This division is also not related to the intensity with which individuals use these objects – for example, a salesperson whose phone is constantly ringing, and a teenager who is constantly messaging with his friends. Instead, the primary aspect is the impact of the obviousness, the untroubled belief that a means of communication is as natural part of our environment as nature itself. The second is the accessibility of memories that things were not always like this. We are dealing with a generational divide that is identical to those created by earlier technologies and objects – its essence is not based on a different attitude towards them by members of different generations or the means of using the media – but rather, in the degree to which we treat them as "black boxes," as things that are simply there without the need for further justification.

Thus, the paradox is that for the youth, telecommunication devices (especially cellphones, mp3 players, networked computers) are not as important as they are for the older generations, because for the former they are so closely bound with everyday practices that their use does not cause reflection, it is not the subject of controversy or negotiations, which would determine the technology's place in the lives of the younger generation. We should keep in mind that this lack of interest in media, their transparency, proves that the characteristic trait of the youth, and their relations with the world, is the fact that their communities are mainly constituted by modern communication technologies, without which (and their close relationship with this generation), it would not be what it currently is.

Marek Krajewski

INTENSITY

How do the young – melded with media-objects –utilize the ability to remain in constant contact, coordination and representation? In this chapter, we show how everyday life becomes more intense when the technologies which allow tele-reachability and tele-presence bring their users into a state of perpetual 'stand-by' status. The physical space of a face to face conversation is augmented by always available communication networks which allow a partial surpassing of time-space limitations on social life. The effect is the experience of connectedness and online-ness – an intensification of the human and social. More and more, the medium of this intensification is the image. Digital photos not only signify existence, but also actively co-create new relations.

Even though direct communications are intertwined with various forms of media remediated communications, our collaborators considered the in-person meeting as the fullest and most fulfilling form of contact. *None of my important relationships progressed thanks to chats or text messages* – says Gośka from Parna, who has no doubt that strength and authenticity in relationships is reachable only through direct contact. An indicator of concern for a relationship is the frequency of contacts. *Each day I meet up with three or four friends, but sometimes, I see twenty, twenty-five people in a day* – she adds.

Thus, we should not be surprised that a large part of the practices related to new-media usage is aimed at creating and taking advantage of opportunities for face to face interactions. Before describing these practices more thoroughly, we should note that their leitmotiv is everyday movement: trips to school, leaving class during breaks, the road home and its detours, visiting favorite places, waiting at the bus-stop and wasting time on a bus stuck in traffic, random meetings out on the town, getting together with friends at planned events, getting lost in concert crowds, trips out of town.... One of the ethnographers noted that in one Friday night, the young people he was with, changed locations three times between two clubs, while "hanging out" on benches two other times. Young people are perpetually on the move, and a necessary condition for the functioning of the social machine is the constant transmission of information about who's where, with whom, and what they are doing.

Coordination of face to face and hand in hand meetings

After the experiment in which we asked her to spend 24 hours without new media, Agata told the ethnographer that she was not able to arrange to meet up with her friend Asia to practice playing djembe after school (djembe is a type of drum). They go to the same school, but Asia was not able to say where she'd be when Agata finished her classes. If it wasn't for the experimental lack of a cell phone, Agata would have simply called Asia, and asked her where she is. This mobility gives the ability to easily react to surprises, obstacles, delays, changes in others' plans, opportunities to do something spontaneously, joining and separating from groups of friends out on the town, but also a chance to effectively use free time when it suddenly appears. However, it is not only an insurance policy if group plans fall apart.

The world of youth and new media, is one where the ability to remain constantly in touch is the norm (to the extent that in Zahaczew, a cellphone network's notification that a customer is "out of range" is nearly synonymous with the person being at "Stocznia" [transl. note: shipyard] – the only bar without network coverage). Because of this, the practices of setting up meet-ups in a set place at a set time are changing. Many of the young people whom we met, agree to meet up near a spot at 'about' a certaintime, rather than specifying the exact time and place.

Gośka from Parna never "wastes time." Thanks to this she gets good grades and can still hang out with a large group of friends, spend time with her boyfriend, make time for her parents, get tutored, go to concerts, parties and other extracurricular activities. She frequently reschedules her meetings but always gives notice and is never late. She knows exactly how much time she has to meet with me, and assertively says: *I gotta go now*, when my time allotted in her schedule runs out – noted the ethnographer who worked with her. Gośka doesn't have a physical calendar, but remembers all her obligations, noting the most important ones in her cellphone. When one event ends sooner than expected, she immediately reaches for her phone, calls a friend whom she's tutoring and moves their appointment, and then reschedules her time with her boyfriend. There's no aimless bumming around, sitting on a bench and smoking a cigarette, or pointlessly waiting.

Such tightly coordinated activities and togetherness are possible thanks to the use of cellphones. After the mobile phone, Gadu-Gadu is the second most important actor in allowing the young to organize their social activities. *When I wanna go out, I turn on my computer, fire up the Gadulec* (transl. note: diminutive nickname for Gadu-Gadu) *and see who's online and who's not. If there are a couple people, a group chat 'what are we doing?' goes out – I'm going to my girlfriend's; I'm free in half an hour; I'm free now, and coming over; check-out what's up with Kuba; Andrzej might come when he finishes up.*

The examples above show how important face to face meetings are for our collaborators. The internet and mobile phones do not change young people into alienated individuals for whom technologically mediated contacts are the basic experience of being with another human being. In fact, physical proximity is a chance to be together, to talk, to experience communally which are all enhanced by the practices of calling, messaging, sending signals and using online communicators.

Constant stand-by

New communication technologies mean that their users live in a state of tele-presence and tele-reachability, which significantly affects their behaviors, the social relations they build with others, as well as, how they treat their own bodies. The mobile phone which can always ring, places its owner in a state of stand-by – writes **Marek Krajewski**, a sociologist at Adam Mickiewicz University in Poznań.

The new telecommunication devices have two unique characteristics which organize their owners' behavior. First, they are constantly present in almost every conceivable situation (due to their progressing miniaturization), second, most of them allow both receiving and sending of signals, as well as recording of images and sounds (for example: every modern cellphone is equipped with a camera, almost every laptop/netbook has similar capacities built in). These two characteristics have numerous social and identity-related consequences. First, they allow both a telepresence and tele-availability of individuals, not just the ones using them but also those around them. Due to this, individuals become omnipotent but are also placed in a state of constant exposure, a readiness to be photographed, filmed, translated into a representation which, once posted online, leads a life of its own. This, in turn, leads to the third point, a tremendous attention to one's external facade, a hyper-expressive mode of behavior, a careful scripting of public 'performances' and the reliance on ready scenarios of physical displays provided by other users of global communication networks. I feel that, today's web, is largely made up of public rehearsals ahead of real performances to be held around those physically present. It is in these terms that we can interpret the "fashion blogger" phenomenon, the presentation of amateur creative efforts on the internet, photos posted on dating websites, and drafts of academic texts, etc. The state of permanent rehearsal, a continuous state of preparations and sketches, of 'un-finishedness' – which appears to be a characteristic of modern culture.

Goffman theorized (which became the basis for seeing social life as a drama) that people behave differently in the presence of others than they do when they are alone and are not observed by others. This mechanism remains valid, but others are now equipped with devices capable of registering each 'performance' and distributing these images or videos, which greatly enlarges the number of potential viewers and increases the possibility of a disconnect between the information which an individual wants to share about themselves, and the ones they actually transmit. These devices, only lead to telenoi among those for whom they are not a natural environment (Ascott 2003: 257-276). For the younger generation, tele-presence and connectedness are basic dimensions of existence, just as natural to their existence, as understanding others' glances, images in the mirror or dimensions of social networks were for previous generations.

As a consequence, bodies become extremely important for the youth, despite the fact that physicality should, at first glance, be undervalued due to it being transferred into a digital representation coursing the internet. Modern telecommunication devices not only force individuals to enter into the state of vigilance and suggest that he exists in a state of continuous exposure, but also become natural extensions of the body, experienced more as its integral part rather than a technological extension. Perfectly fitted to our hands, with a pleasing texture, engaging at least three senses, they respond to our commands like a living organism, making it difficult to find our bodies' boundaries and location. But, they also are an integral part of the modern communication sphere, resulting in our bodies' becoming plugged-in to the networks as just another device. Interestingly, this does not result, as critics claim, in dehumanization but rather, in the intensification of the human and social. When we concede that using tools is a typically human trait, then we are dealing not with a trans-humanism, but rather, with the fulfillment of the typically human-kind specificity of the inseparability of humans and their bodies' technological extensions. This process causes the body to become part of the technological network, to react to its impulses and even generate these impulses. This process allows our bodies to be 'socially' alive, to function by affecting the world, by making a difference. Remaining in the state of vigilance means that an individual exists and experiences only when its organism acts as a router, gathering information and transferring it on, when it is engaged in maintaining the web, of which it is a part. An analogous situation occurs with the objects which allow our bodies to become connected to the web. They are alive and functional only when they connect us with others, when they transfer information and allow it to circulate.

For those terrified at the sight of teenagers intertwined with their computers and mobile phones, and whose fears generate a moral (techno)panic, fed by media tales of anti-social, amoral, barbaric acts committed by teenagers using/under the influence of/in relation to these types of devices, there are a few important facts to consider:

First, most of these devices fulfill modernist fantasies (fulfilling the hopes of grandparents, great-grandparents and parents) of means which would allow us to overcome the limitations of our bodies, locating the youth in the 'dreams of others," in a world developed and thought out by its current critics.

Second, current communication technologies are in a position similar to other technological advances, which used to cause moral panic. For example, Sławomir Magala wrote about concerns surrounding the installation of the first telephones in private apartments in Vienna: "...most of the disputes surrounding their installation dealt with anticipated problems with scandalous behavior. There was a debate on how to avoid situations in which the lady of the house would be spoken to by an unknown man [...]. To avoid this terrifying eventuality, it was agreed that a servant would answer the phone, and she would hand it to the lady once she determined that the caller was someone *comme il faut*" (Magala 1999: 19-20).

Third, **today's telecommunication devices hold a great potential for bolstering socialization, they are, in fact, machines for creating bonds** and relations, and the only thing to fear is the excess of opportunities and social choices which they offer. This means that social relation networks were never as dense as they are today, and never before has technology eliminated so many time, space, social class, political and cultural divisions as today. Of course, this does not create a state of universal solidarity, love, profound and strong bonds, the desire to cooperate or become civically engaged, but it definitely socializes – it creates the pretexts, means and platforms for creating interpersonal bonds. This potential socialization, built into communication devices makes them popular and is one of the main reasons why the young remain in a state of vigilance.

Is it then surprising that these modern devices, which can be referred to as objects-media (see Krajewski, 2008), have built in interactive functions which suggested communication even when there is no one on the other side? A telephone can be voice-activated, it can say and show where we are, store our friends' voices, photos and films of our meetings with them, and thanks to the phonebook we have all of our friends available and contact with them is always possible. Even when none of our friends is available, we can at least send a text message to a contest and someone/something will definitely answer. When I listen to music, the player tells me what I'm listening to, and suggests when I can buy the album or song, connects me to others listening to the same thing, they are close to me but I do not know them at all, but can read their opinions and comments. The device confirms that I exist. I exist because I act, because the effects are visible in the form of online activities or, at least, potential interactions in the telecommunication networks.

Marek Krajewski

New dimensions of contacts

In describing the intensification of being together, we have shown the dimension of practices surrounding face to face meetings arranged through new media. In this section we describe practices of togetherness, which are not only aided, but actually only possible due to mobile phones and the internet. By calling each other, sending text messages, sending signals, chatting on communicators, blogging or talking on social networking sites, the young maintain intense contacts even when they are physically separate.

When Klara goes home after school, a friend walks her to the bus stop to Małe Lutki. They discuss the day's news. When Klara gets home, she eats something and briefly watches TV. Then, *I sit down at the computer, check my mail, check out the school's website*. Checking her favorite web sites does not take long:

Kominek.blox.pl, Pajacyk, Last.fm, Onet...When she starts doing homework her computer is still on. *I like listening to music when I do homework, and I always have Gadu turned on, so I can always chat somebody up.* That somebody is usually her friend. *We can talk for three hours on Gadu. We start with school, and then each of us tells some story, we chat about what we did over the weekend, I don't know where the time goes.* In the evenings the girls carry on several conversations (as many as seven or eight) at the same time, but one is always between the two of them. There's always something to discuss, even if they just saw each other at the bus stop.

Intensive electronic contacts with physically distant people maintains relationships, or sometimes even saves them from oblivion. Kamila from Zahaczewo misses her friend Helenka, who moved to England. Her friendship with Helenka used to take up most of her time – they used to do just about everything together. They still have shared plans for the future, but daily contact through the internet is difficult. Mostly because its hard for them to find time and arrange online meetings. Their daily routines are different, and the time difference is a big obstacle in the evenings. They maintain contact through Skype, Facebook and email. Unlike most of her friends, Kamila writes a lot of emails – a mode of communication they find marginal and rather formal. Emails between Helenka and Kamila take the form of 'classic' letters, divided into paragraphs. The friends discuss events and clarify details from previous letters. They chat on Skype less frequently, but when they do get together, they talk for hours, while making tea, cleaning and reading other things and listening to music. Kamila doesn't have headphones so *Helenka is coming through the speakers.* This is why Kamila wants a laptop, to take it to her room upstairs and talk "normally." Such a use of communication technologies encourages reflexivity in relations, due to the automatically archived, changing texts (we discuss reflexive uses of technology in the "Technologies of reflexiveness" chapter on p. 50).

Relationships also develop through getting to know each other's interests, views, adventures, doubts. A good example of this is Marianna's blog, which, according to Iza: *Marianna writes really well, I really liked it, she wrote about her beliefs, ideology, I don't know what to call it, I just liked it, it was something to discuss.* The fact that Marianna had a blog came out in a general conversation about blogs, what they like to read, and then Marianna mentioned that she had a blog and gave the address to Iza. *I used to check it out every other day, to see what was new,* recalls Iza. *Now I go there everyday and see if Marianna wrote something.* (Marianna no longer writes her blog – after her boyfriend's complaints, who thought that she included too many intimate details about their relationship).

The ability to contact each other by mobile phone or communicator allows the maintenance of relationships, especially when face to face contacts are rarer. It is clear that the practices of using technologies allow an elastic and specific support where it is needed, with a simultaneous lack of mediated contacts, if face to face interactions are adequately frequent. Gosia rarely uses Gadu-Gadu with her roommates. *With some of my very good friends, I sporadically talk on GG, because the intensity of our meetings is such, that it is no longer necessary.* At the same time she very frequently uses it to interact with an elementary school friend. *We're up to date with each other thanks to GG, even though we rarely see each other and don't have mutual friends.* In Gosia's relationship GG is a better, cheaper (than the phone) means of communicating.

The intensification of contacts enhances what can be colloquially called the smoothing out language issues. At issue here is the feeling that the communication is successful, that both sides understand and send appropriate signals, along with intentions and subtleties such as humor and irony. This is particularly significant when a group is created through intense communication (direct and remediated), and not through references to elements of identity.

It is important to note that our collaborators experienced these contacts as stable and authentic friendships despite the limitations (lack of sound or visual elements) imposed by various communication devices. Gośka and her friends unanimously agree on the importance of reading gestures and facial expressions. Comfort in contacts remediated by media can only be reached, if the knowledge of the other person is good enough that one can imagine their behavior. With people who are close to us, we can feel the tone of voice, facial expressions and gestures just like we do live, says Gośka.

All of these observations and conversations convinced us that, for our collaborators, direct contacts as well as remediated ones are indivisible, they are part of the same social space. We noticed that activities occurring in the physical realm extend into the net, and the reverse. Contact with friends is a common theme with all of these media, not just the obvious ones such as using mobile phones. This is also the case for examples less clearly associated with communication, such as ones which are part of the third dimension of intensification of being together – the exchange of media texts. Among the high school students we met, the ever-present cellphones take a back seat to a different type of device: the camera.

To be is to take photos

Krzysiek, *Młody*, and Alek are just three of the Ziemielin crew, for whom photography is a primary way of spending time. The girls from Zahaczewo, when bored, started to meet up for photo shoots which are fun for both the photographer and the 'models'. On her desktop, Gośka from Parna has a photo of her boyfriend Piotrek's band. We were surprised to find out how important photography was for the youth we met as part of this project. Along with music, it was the primary hobby we found (see p. 89). Moreover, it was not only a hobby but also a part of the everyday practices of social life. This expansion of the significance of images in the lives of the youth is very significant and is not fully explained by the affordability (free) of taking photos with a digital camera, and the presence of cameras in nearly all mobile phones. This is clearly visible in the importance of photos in intensifying experiences of togetherness. The young are not only consumers of images, but also their creators, and, very frequently, their objects – when they pose for each other.

In the field we met young people for whom images were a means of communication just like text. Of course, it would be a mistake to only analyze culture's visual aspects, because – as W.J.T. Mitchell (2005) noted critically – there are no solely visual media. All media are mixed – their broadcasting and reception is connected to other senses besides sight such as hearing and touch. However, we cannot overlook the unprecedented rise in the production of images and the filling of the world with photos, non-photographic images and visual representations. Photographing was never as cheap and easy, or as common and frequent as it is now. Just about anyone can take photos, and everyone is exposed to a flood of visual signals. The young people we met while working on this project communicate through images skillfully and frequently. Digital cameras – as separate devices or built into cellphones are omnipresent. We also worked with high school students who used analog cameras, and then converted their photos into digital files. Photos taken by the young, regardless of the technology used to produce them, take on their full meaning only after they're brought into digital circulation, where they are easily copied, edited and shared.

This saturation with photographs and imagery and the general ability to create, modify and present photography does not mean that there are more photographers or photographic talents than in previous years. Photography is involved in many everyday practices not connected directly with art or other conventional uses of photographs (journalism, documentation, commemoration).

In the lives of our young collaborators photos play an interesting performative function as well – photographing allows the establishment and maintenance of interpersonal bonds: **photos not only record things, but also do things**. Photos are also communication tools – they let people show their environments, who they are (many of our collaborators have an incredible awareness of the medium – when a camera is pointed at them, they assume poses nearly instinctively), and who 'they are with.' Let us take a look at these roles.

Photographs are more direct, and "a picture is worth a thousand words." This is why they are frequently used as an aid in communication. When Iza from Ziemielin was looking for an eighteenth birthday present for Marianna, she settled on a basket for her friend's bicycle. Iza and her friends had to figure out which basket to buy, for how much and what their contribution would be. Finally, Iza spotted a basket she liked at a store in town, and decided that her friend would like it. To show the basket to others, and have her choice approved – she found it on Allegro (transl. note: Polish online auction platfom, similar to eBay) and sent her friends the link. Everyone agreed. The above story shows how a photo can be used share knowledge. Images guarantee clarity and ensure obviousness. In times when more and more situations require coordination mediated by electronic communications, a photo reduces the risk of misunderstanding a simple message. When one friend asks another (on Gadu-Gadu): *which dress did you buy?* the answer is usually a jpg file or a link to it.

Wiktor, Kuba's friend from Zahaczewo, lives with his grandparents because his parents moved to England for work. After the school year ended, he visited them for a summer job and vacation. His friend Monika went with him. Talking about this experience, Kuba shows us Wiktor's profile on Nasza-klasa. To his surprise, Wiktor's profile picture was now a photo of him and Monika. Kuba is clearly shocked, but also completely convinced this is no accident – a picture together on a Nasza-klasa profile is a public announcement that Wiktor and Monika are a couple. As Kuba explains, if it was just one of the photos in an online album, people would wonder if they were together. But, a profile picture is a "public face" – changes to it are a big deal. From their hometown friends' perspective, Wiktor and Monika became a couple through this very photograph.

Beyond informational purposes, photos play more subtle and complex roles as well. Primarily, they provide means for self-expression. The ability to express themselves is intensely used by the youth. Being with them and observing their everyday life, we felt that there are few things more important to them than "being creative" (we discuss the issue more in "Geeking out" – p. 113). Expressing oneself is most powerfully transmitted creatively through passions but is also possible through simple processes such as stylizing simple everyday objects, surroundings, outfits, and even events into unique and uncommon ones (we write more about style in "Aestheticizing" p. 78). This is the reason behind decorating rooms, collecting things – from bottles on a shelf to blogs in browser tabs. Photography gives opportunity to express oneself, to be creative. Nearly all the young people we met either took photos or posed for their friends' photos. *I have an inner need to create* – Krzysiek, a passionate photographer, told us – *I'm most comfortable creating images.* In his case, a casual interest in taking photos became a serious passion and part of his future plans. Krzysiek, like many of the high school students with whom we spoke, wants to work in a creative field. After school, he wants to study photography in Opava in the Czech Republic.

One can also use photography to function in the everyday. Photos are not only used to express emotions, but also to experience and create them. The boundary between actions and expressions is becoming blurred, because, for the youth, photos play an integral role in the world they experience. Similarly, the boundary between an event and its digital representation is also fading away – which allows us to talk about their performative aspects. With photos, one can not only express something, but can also do something specific with them. Using a photo, one can like someone or not, love someone, remember someone, hurt someone or insult them.

Photos, it is worth noting, are also an instrument of memory, and integral part of the practices of remembering and reminiscing. *This year we went on a school trip to Prague. Unfortunately I broke my leg. I took photos to remember* – explains Alek. Gośka tells us about a photo showing her friends asleep: *This was after our first* outdoor party. Some people fell asleep, and the others talked about life and death until 7 a.m. I have very warm memories of that time. This photo-memory is consciously built. A camera and the ability to photograph fundamentally change young people's perception of time. **Thanks to the ability to reflecxively plan-out memories the young people's horizon of the future is changing. Agata, going to a party, knows and announces: there will be photos – meaning that there will be memories.**

Photographic sociability and remediating memory

Mateusz Halawa: The second I saw it, I fell in love with this photo. It's very sensual, looking at it I can feel the happiness, the heat, youth and the sensation of freedom.

I like how it captures movement – the quintessence of photography. This is what taking pictures is about – capturing a moment, preserving it from oblivion. There you are: with friends, happy, suspended in the air. ("Taking pictures of people jumping is basically the reason photography was invented," a friend once commented one of my "jumping" photos posted on Facebook). The only thing that matters is the moment now – nothing else. Still, this "now" moment also appears to be already past. When I look at this photo I can not help but feel nostalgic. Perhaps its something to do with the ORWO colors (a former East German manufacturer of films), maybe the slight blurriness, but looking at it I know I'm looking at an artifact of the past.

It is this tension between the "now" and "then" which caught my eye. I paused over this photo, while looking at hundreds of others for this report, and chose it, for my consideration of memories, media and identity.

If we were to add Krzysiek, who took the photo, we'd have the whole Ziemielin crew which went to the lake on the last day of vacation to hang out, jump into the water, drink beer and take pictures. There's Iza, *Młody*, Anie, Grzesiu, Tomek and Alek... There's summer 2009.

Krzysiek is standing in the water, directing the scene so that everyone would be synchronized in the air. In his hand is a cheap waterproof disposable camera, but you can see he's a skilled photographer. (We got the picture from his photo-blog. He scanned the negative and didn't want to remove the hair which got caught between the scanner and the lens – which is the white mark on the photo). The choice of this analog and unique old-school low-fi aesthetic was a conscious choice, as was the photo's composition (Digital cameras were available but were not used.) Making this photo happen took some work, but was also a lot of fun.

Their day trip to the lake was aimed at spending time together and taking photos. This picture is not only a record of them being together – they are together through taking each other's photos. Their friendship can be photographed (it can be represented through technology, in this sense, "being friends" is not only a form of relationship, but also a certain visual category, which our collaborators skillfully manipulate), but it also exists through the act of taking photos. In this moment, being together is taking photographs and being photographed; this moment is both togetherness and a photo shoot.

This picture reminds me of various forms of remediation which are taking place here. (But it also doesn't let its joy be pummeled by over-theorizing, the joy radiates – drops of water slowly drying out in the sun.) What we've got is the experience of being together by the lake mediated by the camera. We've got a photo – arranged, taken, developed, scanned and posted online in a digital form. The photo itself becomes the medium of friendship both online and off.

I'm sending the photo on to José van Dijck, because we're dealing here with the subject of his latest book – the remediation of memory – which involve "activities and objects we produce and appropriate by means of media technologies for creating and re-creating a sense of our past, present, and future selves in relation to others" (2007: 107-171).

An everyday digital (or digitized) photo thus becomes a "technology of the self" (Foucault 2000: 247-293).

José van Dijck: This photo illustrates the highest form of photographic sociability: through this photo friendship is established and communicated; in essence, it is in the act of photographing that the bond is realized.

Taking photos is a mediated action, whose results are mediated memories, while its function is both communicative and archival. Jumping into a lake with friends is obviously a social event, but taking photos of it changes it into an activity with intended results: it encloses friendship into the frames of memory.

By sharing and distributing the photo online, these friends create a feeling of the present, which, at any point in the future, can by transformed into an experience of the past.

LOVE

New communication technologies, such as mobile phones, skype or photoblogs, are affecting intimate relationships. Media become intimate, when a mediated relationship with another person is experienced as close and authentic. At the same time, network logic dilutes the hard divisions between private and public. A new form of semi-public or private-public life, where privacy can be publicized, and by marshalling the public network's functions and resources, make the internet an intimate, personal space.

Six photos. Each with the same scenery – a cast iron structure of an old bridge. The sky is blue, the day sunny – the middle of a hot summer. Between the bridge's cast iron beams there's a dark-haired girl. In one, she looks up, in one she looks to the side, as if she didn't realize the camera's there. Looking at her, you can almost feel the fresh air which she's breathing and the slight breeze blowing through her long hair. She's looking straight at the camera, leaning on a bannister. She's frozen in a pose found in various fashion shoots.

Twelve photos. All arranged the same way. In all, a common scenery – a forest. In all, the same young woman. She looks in the camera, smiles, makes a thoughtful face, lowers her head and makes a sad face. In one picture she's holding a red rose. It's fall. A few weeks after we met Agata and Karol from Ziemielin. Agata is the model, Karol the photographer. *I'm used to posing* – Agata tells us – *Karol takes a lot of photos of me.* Puts them on a blog and signs: "my muse," "for the most important person in my life," "thanks, Kotuś (trans. kitten)."

Love in the age of digital media

In this report, love functions as a specific subgroup of "being together." We met a few couples who were "in love" – besides Karol and Agata, there was Gośka and Piotrek, *Młody* and Ania, Marianna and Jurek and Kamila and Bartek. We asked ourselves whether love affects how they use media, and if media affect their love. What does it mean to be in love, to have a boyfriend or girlfriend, to be in a relationship in the era of new media?

Understandably, couples in love place an even higher premium on face to face and hand to hand interactions (over mediated contacts) than people who know each other or are simply friends. As Olka Gołdys wrote in her description of the day in which she met Gośka's boyfriend: "They are as intertwined as only high school lovers can be, constantly stroking each other, hidden in themselves, with limbs twisted together so that you do not know who's hand or foot is whose. The primacy of touch (an innocent and subtle form of it) is so clear, that I could not imagine them being satisfied with Gadu-Gadu emoticons or a Skype chat." The couple tries to spend every free moment together, during the school year there's little free time between school, homework, extracurriculars, helping parents – all these activities imposed on them by the outside world take up most of their days. Media allow the lovers to challenge these limits. The limits imposed on them by the adult world, daily schedules or physical distance.

An asymmetric balance

In a romantic relationship contacts and media usage is much more intense than in normal togetherness situations, and is often asymmetric. On the other hand, the ability to stay in contact over distances is used by couples much more intensely than by people in other types of close relationships. With this, comes another issue – media can become romantic artifacts.

The materialization of communication processes which constitute a relationship can cause a text message to become a keepsake of a declaration of love. New media give entirely new possibilities to learn about one another and cement one's relationship. Young people constantly send each other cultural objects like music, movies, and photos which are significant to them and which are important designators of their identities. That which is stored on their computers is even more readily available for sharing. The internet allows the learning of their partners "media diets" and lets them revisit websites which are significant to the other. Karol, for example, is interested in the cultural activities of a local squat – Agata regularly checks the commune's website to stay current with its activities, and to show her boyfriend that what is important to him is also significant for her.

Agata and Karol are together virtually everyday. Their relationships is relatively new – they've been together for three months – the "newness" of a relationship is relative. Three months might be perceived as a long time in a first 'serious' relationship – at the same time, other couples, such as Marianna and Jurek have been together much longer). Communication technologies allow them to coordinate their time. Karol constantly calls Agata. To ask where she is, to agree to meet up somewhere and when they can be together. Of course, this coordinating calling is not an exclusive feature of romantic relationships. High schoolers we met use similar means to coordinate meetings with various friends. However, there is a fundamental difference: partners are people with whom constant coordination is necessary. The lovers can be in different physical spaces, but they cannot not know where the other is and what she's doing. In this context, love is a type of a commitment – it requires much more attention to be paid much more frequently than in less intimate relationships. Just how significant this commitment is, becomes clear in Marianna's statement that she doesn't particularly enjoy sending a text messages, but sends more than a dozen to her boyfriend each day. At school, she does so during every break between periods. As can be deduced from the frequency of these communications, these text messages do not always contain the most significant information, in fact, they rarely do. Usually, they are simply an expression of the ever-implied "I'm thinking of you."

A mobile phone allows an ongoing sharing of what's going on, what's important. Karol, who went to the doctor's on the day of the 'no new media' experiment, noted that he wanted to message Agata and his Mom *"everything's ok – I'm healthy."* The need to remain in constant contact sometimes clashes with limited financial means. This is why, Agata, who has more minutes in her mobile phone plan than Karol, takes over the responsibility for the majority of their contacts when her boyfriend lacks funds on his mobile phone. The phone also softens the pain of being apart. Agata recalls: *the most I ever paid for my phone was when I was at the sea, that's when we spoke the most (with Karol).* In this instance, love suspends, to some extent, the cardinal rule of reciprocity. In no other relationship is it conceivable that one would make more calls, than receive them. In other relationships, the balance between incoming and outgoing connections must be balanced.

When Karol doesn't call for a longer period of time (the question of what constitutes 'longer' is relative and is determined through negotiations within the relationship), Agata does not hesitate to call him on her own. She does not assume bad intentions on his part, or a desire to use up her minutes, she believes that he doesn't call because he can not afford it. The asymmetry in the exchange of attention, which is not tolerated in non-intimate relationships, is the norm in romantic ones (This was confirmed in group interviews we conducted.) Such a procedure was popular among the couples we met, but was not used in other types of relationships.

Getting closer while apart

Communication technologies are not only useful for those for whom physical distance is a sporadic issue (for example during vacations), but also when distance is a permanent obstacle. This is the case with Marianna and Jurek – they live in towns 80 kilometers apart. Even though Jurek, who is older, has a car, they cannot see each other everyday. They maintain contact largely through Skype conversations which are cheaper than the ones on the phone. Their long talks usually happen in the evenings – to provide greater intimacy, he bought Marianna earphones and a microphone. When Marianna goes to bed, she brings her laptop along and starts talking with Jurek. This summer, she worked as a waitress at a restaurant so that she could buy a laptop (in our teenagers world, a laptop's main asset is that it can be transported within apartment, taking such an expensive machine outside would be too dangerous). Magda got her laptop from her parents a few months after her boyfriend moved to England with his parents. Because she was spending many hours sitting awkwardly in front of the desktop computer, her parents decided to buy a portable one for her.

Romantic artifacts

Still, it is not the laptop which is the most romantically-linked device used by young people, but rather the ever-present cellphone. A mobile phone is not only a communication device, but also an object which materializes this communication (frequently in the form of text messages), and stores the couples' important memories. *You don't send me these types of text messages anymore* – Agata told Karol with regret in her voice – suggesting that their relationship had become routine. During the new media abstinence experiment, Agata noted that she wanted to read a text message she received the day before, and also that she was waiting for a message. When asked about the personal losses connected to losing a cellphone, the young people listed losing romantic text messages and photos as one of the biggest fears. This is why Gośka from Parna writes down certain (presumably significant) messages from her boyfriend into a notebook. Transferred onto a piece of paper, these electronic words are left to dry on paper.

Young people do not just exchange photos and text messages. Since love is the most intense form of being together, it also intensifies matters which are significant to social groupings. Among them is the sharing of media materials – a crucial aspect of social groups. In this case, the purpose is not just circulating cultural texts or giving a friend a movie or record which might interest them. The other purpose is to get to know each other better. Watching movies and listening to music together has always been one of the main ways in which people spend time together. In her musical searches, Gośka was largely inspired by the music given to her by a friend who wanted to get closer to her.

Marianna enjoys watching *House* with Jurek. However, the young watch this show differently than their parents did with their favorite shows – Jurek downloads episodes from the internet, and they use a laptop screen rather than a TV to watch. Of course, spending time together and meshing cultural reference catalogues and incorporating them into their intimate communications remains paramount (The importance of which was experienced by Marianna's friend Alek, who still recalls talking with a newly met girl, and not being able to correctly interpret any of her pop-culture references – the risk of this is greatly increased in the era of the internet.) The closer we analyze this shared time spent before the computer screen, the more we are able to notice the differences in cultural consumption practices brought on by the internet and computers. The seemingly obvious differences between content accessed through the computer (ability to personally select the text and the time of its 'showing') contrasts with options offered by cinema, television and radio, and leads to less obvious aspects of shared consumption.

Piotrek freqently sends me links to music videos on YouTube – explains Gośka. When she shows the anthropologist she's working with a video from her computer she says: *I got this song from Piotrek by Gadu*. Spending time together in front of the computer is a practice which affects a relationship more than watching TV together. Gośka recalls that after a concert *together, we searched for the song by its lyrics*. Young people can present their media-worlds to their partners by sharing favorite movies, songs, or photos, but also by guiding them through larger parts of the internet like services, portals and forums. They can do so when together, or remotely – by sending digital gifts which either help understand their passions, or demonstrate their closeness through knowledge of the recipient's tastes and preferences (In this way, a link sent on Gadu-Gadu can illustrate the strength of their bond, by showing that the sender understands what the recipient will like.)

This is another example of how digital media materializes and externalizes processes which, in the analog world, remained largely unconscious. Passions become archived and shared. Mutual interests are no longer abstract constructs, but rather materialize as bookmarks in browsers or playlists on mp3 players. Even if surfing the net together is somewhat like channel surfing from the same couch, it is even more similar to showing someone around your town, and sharing favorite places with someone close to you. This increased freedom not only affects the presentation of the self and sharing – it also allows for a better knowledge of the partner without his or her direct participation. The digital wold makes it easier to follow the footsteps of a loved one. Agata follows Karol's photoblog, visits pages he finds interesting or sites which feature his photos. If you love someone, you add their important web addresses to your own browser. This way, a public space like the internet, woven into an intimate relationship, becomes the glue that holds the most private relationships together.

An intimate internet

Młody has been with ania for two years, and for the last two years he's taken pictures of her everyday. He takes pictures everyday anyway, but those of Ania are special. Each day they show up on a blog, which is only accessible to the two of them. All of their close friends know about it, but nobody's seen them.

The seemingly public and global space of the internet, is consciously and carefully scaled to the size of an intimate love relationship. *Młody* made sure that the blog and its content was not displayed on web-searches, and was only accessible to him and Ania. The url address is their secret. The most important part of it are photos – which illustrate the feelings that bind them. It is a diary of their relationship, proof of an intimate relationship. Sometimes, it requires him to wake up early and meet up with Ania before school. Since *Młody* lives on the edge of town and sometimes misses his bus, he occasionally has to catch her wherever she is – like the school cafeteria. Sometimes, he waits for her until it's very late.

While their photos are on the net, nobody besides them can access these photos. In *Młody* and Ania's relationship, a global communication network becomes an intimate medium, open to just the two lovers. This is an example of how the internet can be scaled through use of practices. The manner in which the couple uses the internet shows that relationships mediated through new media can remain far removed from the exhibitionism frequently ascribed to them. After all, *Młody's* website is only for him and Ania. The experience of sharing something as a couple, a space that is their own, and remains invisible to the rest of the world is extremely important in young people's relationships. They rarely have access to a completely personal physical space, "their own" places, almost always remaining within the controlling sight of the adults.

The use of the web in relationships is not always similar to Ania and *Młody*'s. However, it is rarely a completely public environment. It can be described as semi-public, because even if they are accessible on the "open internet" their proper interpretation is only possible with detailed knowledge of the social context: who's dating whom, what happened at the party or inside jokes understood only by friends. With couples, these types of texts are addressed to friends and acquaintances, for whom they often represent something akin to public manifestos.

Within the semi-public sphere, text (not just images) is also significant. Marianna had a blog when she was with her former boyfriend. When she started seeing Jurek, she abandoned it and started a new one. For Jurek, the situations she described in it were too intimate for public consumption. Marianna, stopped writing it. She did it – as she explained – for the sake of the relationship. Semi-public can also signify a channel of communication. On Gadu-Gadu we could see Maga and her boyfriend's changing status messages: "I'm sad," "I'm also sad," "nobody writes to me," "maybe he's afraid to write," "somebody made me sad," "somebody feels dumb." These statuses are public, many people can see them, but, to correctly interpret them we need to have mutual friends and understand the context. It is not enough to literally read these statements. In order too really understand them, it is necessary to know the context which reaches well beyond what is wrongly referred to as the "virtual" world.

TECHNOLOGIES OF REFLEXIVITY

New media are both tools of socialization and individualization: they mediate the development of new types of communities, while participating in the establishment of unique forms of "self." In this chapter we describe how, by participating in the identity creation processes, new communication technologies become "technologies of the self." an important element of this is reflexivity – by materializing fleeting thoughts, emotions and contacts into searchable databases, digital media encourage personal growth, which engages with feedback flowing from the web.

The practices of internet and mobile phone use which we observed lead us to believe that **new media architecture causes an increase in individuals' reflexive actions.** This reflexiveness appears in two forms which we discuss in this chapter. First is a reflexivity directed toward functioning in social environments. It deals directly with relationships, recognizes their value and potential and problematizes both the depth and breadth of contacts. The second type of reflexiveness is one based on developing the 'self.' They are both inextricably intertwined with each other, and their division is purely an analytical device. The digital traces which are constantly left behind are not dusty forgotten archives. They are not static and do not exist in a vacuum. The shape of social life which they reproduce or co-create never settles into a set form. These traces are perpetually renewed and refreshed -- meaning they cooperate in the reflexive development of the 'self.'

Trading attention, or how social networks materialize glances

One of the most obvious examples of increased reflexiveness of practices related to new media are social networking websites. Counting friends (and friends of friends), searching the database, materializing temporary contacts, discovering unexpected connections, archiving of relationship-building gestures are some of the most prominent and almost-necessary functions of sites such as Nasza-klasa or Facebook (see p. 83). As a result of these actions, users become conscious of their potential to create connections online. Even if this potential is not converted into actions, it is significant that through participating on the internet, a unique form of experiencing the self as part of a network is born. A feedback loop, typical of these types of reflexive actions, takes place between actions and observations. "Machines for creating bonds and relations," as Marek Krajewski wrote in this report (p. 56), are also machines for observing, measuring and manipulating these bonds and relations. The fact that reflexiveness is largely based on observing (showing oneself, making oneself open to others' comments, the resulting consciousness of being seen and of observing others who are similarly presenting themselves for public viewing), is extremely important and connected structurally to process which go far beyond technology or media – the processes of aestheticizing the everyday (see p. 78).

A street in Ziemielin. Our collaborator Marianna runs into Marek, a friend she hasn't seen in a long time, with whom she worked during the summer. Marek begins telling her that he just got back from a trip to the Tatra Mountains, but Marianna – suggesting that she follows his online posts – interrupts him: *I know, I saw the pictures on Nasza-klasa.* Marek asks her if she commented on any of them, and Marianna says she hasn't. *No?! Then comment on them!*

This is a characteristic example of how important **semi-public exchanges of attention** are to the young people we met. Marianna made it clear to her friend that she was interested in what's going on his Nasza-klasa profile, but only did so on the street – in a way invisible to Marek's friends online. Judging by his reaction, he wants online evidence that he is liked, that his friends are interested in his life. Investing a few seconds to write such a comment is proof of this fondness. When we discussed the incident with Marianna, her opinions were mixed. On one hand, she thought Marek's actions were too ostentatious, coming dangerously close to obsessive self promotion on a social network. The young people we met often dismissed such tactics, but we observed that they frequently participated in such attention-trading activities, perhaps only limited to a closer group of friends.

Our collaborators mocked *makebelieveland and imaginary friends* – or practices involving maximizing the number of friends on social networks through the inclusion of 'friends' with whom one did not actually know. "Meeting" people on the internet, luring them with 'dramatically low-cut dresses' or 'grotesquely exposed muscles,' was dismissed by everyone we met. Only "authentic" comments were tolerated, but the boundaries of this "authenticity" were never clearly articulated.

Marianna's classmate Alek discussed "inauthentic" contacts this way: *Nasza-klasa tells you when its somebody's birthday. If it's today – it tells you so and so has a birthday today. This way, the shitty friends, who don't really know you, see you have a birthday and send you best wishes on Nasza-klasa, wishing you all the best for ever and ever and so on. But, saying 'happy birthday' is the path of least resistance. Often there are situations where someone will write something on your wall, or let's say Person X writes "happy birthday, best wishes" on person Y's wall, and when they see each other that day he doesn't remember to other has a birthday that day. You know, you look at Nasza-klasa – so you say: 'happy birthday.' Then you see them and ...nothing.*

However, a story Marianna told us shows that while too many comments can be mocked ironically, a lack of any comments is a true problem. Marianna's eight year old niece is a social outcast in her class, she's not liked and doesn't have friends. Her classmates let her know this not only at school, but also on Nasza-klasa. Photos she posts on the site are pointedly left comment-free. Here, we're dealing with the same mechanism as in Marek's example but in reverse: in a world where visible interest from others is one of the symptoms of a group's acceptance, a lack of comments is a manifestation of rejection. It also shows the semi-public nature of social networking websites' dynamic – while everyone (including the girl's parents) can see her profile and take a look at her photos, only her classmates understand that, in this context, the lack of comments below their photos is not simply that, but also a *de facto* social ostracism.

In Lev Manovich's *The Practice of Everyday (Media) Life*, comments and other tokens of interest in other people displayed online by friends are referred to as **gifts**. "What kind of gift you get is less important than the act of getting a gift, or posting a comment or a picture," he writes, noting that the internet changed the social ecosystem (2008). Manovich quotes Adrian Chen who wrote that: "All cultures practice the exchange of tokens that bear and carry meanings, communicate interest and count as personal and social transactions. [...] [These practices are marked] by ambiguity of intent and motive (the token's meaning may be codified while the user's motive for using it may not.) This can double up the meaning of interaction and communication, allowing the recipients of tokens to respond to the token or to the user behind its use" (2008).

The significance of these practices has been altered by social networking services, which translated fleeting manifestations of interest and fondness – a few words exchanged, a quick glance, a smile, or small gesture in a non mediated world – into something permanent, searchable and indexed. Obviously, in an analog world, these gestures were noticeable only in the moment and usually only by their recipient. Nasza-klasa allows a user to see the 'guests' who visited his or her profile – this is a recorded parallel to a glance. Similarly, comments on a photo prove that someone was looking at them – the comment's message is usually immaterial or not as significant as its existence. (We must admit that this evolution has enormously helped in our recruitment of collaborators for this project. We wanted to reach people with diverse and wide social networks. Looking at the mostly public profiles on Nasza-klasa we were able to see not only the number of friends, but also pictures from parties, the number of comments added – the exchange of social 'gifts' was a great help in reaching potential collaborators.

Technologies such as Nasza-klasa materialize glances and in this way, they are changing the basic, sensory dimensions of everyday life. "The union and interaction of individuals is based upon mutual glances," wrote sociologist Georg Simmel (2006 [1921]: 188). According to him, "no objective trace of this relationship is left behind, as is universally found, directly or indirectly, in all other types of associations between men, [...] [Eye to eye interaction] dies in the moment in which the directness of the function is lost." (2006 [1921]: 188) The new, online dimensions of sociability, such as blogs, photoblogs and Nasza-klasa profiles, materialize what was previously not materializeable. Even the briefest comment to a photo posted on Nasza-klasa is a material trace of a glance, just like a statistical record on Last.fm is a material trace of a listen. Thanks to these new technologies senses leave traces. Exchanging comments below Nasza-klasa photos can also be seen as an exchange of glances – placing, supporting and affecting within social relation frames. Among our collaborators, regularly checking each other out in party pictures or amateur photo shoots, the new media-mediated social networks are a new platform where they can be noticed by the people they care about. Maintaining relationships through new media is not only an empty substitute of direct contacts, but a new form of being together. The communication architecture which lets people leave fingerprints (eye-prints?) on friends' profiles, intensifies social life, and stretches social proximity into the online world where an eye to eye glance does not reach.

Aestheticizing the everyday, or why life must have a vibe

Karol's room does not look as if he spends a lot of time there. There are – seemingly – random pieces of furniture. The walls do not have posters, like we'd seen in his friends' rooms. There doesn't appear to be much attention to detail, as if the occupant didn't care if the pillows match the bed cover, or the desk matched the dresser. It is as if functionality was the only thing that mattered, and style and appearances played no role. Style and appearance are very important – just differently expressed. Karol has a couple dreadlocks on top of his head, wears a black t-shirt with a "Dirty Harry" design and sneakers. When our photographer arrived in Ziemielin, he takes him and the ethnographer, along with his girlfriend to the Parking Tower – a seven story unfinished structure in the center of town. It is a graffiti-covered gray concrete labyrinth of huge empty rooms, narrow hallways and stairs, with massive unsecured window openings.

It is a raw and mysterious place, illegal and industrial, punk and exclusive at the same time. Posing for the photographer Tomek Ratter in the Tower interiors, Karol anticipates the style and effect which he senses and helps create. He wants to check out Tomek's famous Mamiya camera. When he gets his hands on it, he takes this photo.

When Karol and his girlfriend are posing for photos, they do not seem to be self-conscious at all. Being photographed does not take them out of their comfort zone, it is a natural, obvious and trained process. They want their feelings to be photographed inside the Tower, so they kiss passionately for precisely as much time as Tomek needs to set up a shot and take a photo. After the shutter snaps, they stop kissing as abruptly as they started. When the photographer says: 'Let's do something like an album cover now,' they quickly work with him to arrange a new scene – her in the foreground, standing straight looking in the camera dressed in jeans and a dark shirt. He's in the background, below her – where the gray stairs end. He's looking off to the side. They're posing for a type of photo they know very well. They know the vibe, the feel the photographer is going for. Knowing what an "album cover" looks like means assuming the right pose and picking the right background.

Gośka spoke a lot about the unity between the visual and sound spheres. The girl not only notices the commonality of the visual sphere (the musician's image) and musical one (the type of music he plays). In fact, she uses these two systems as keys to finding the right songs. Olka Gołdys noted that: In conversations about music (with Gośka) there is a beautiful synesthesia, she searches for reflections or harmony between a musician's sound and her image. Music, outfits, haircuts, or even diet (some of our collaborators were proud and conscious vegetarians), the reason why I take photos, the things that move me – all of this is, to some extent, a question of style. Karol knows how an album cover looks. Like Gośka, who can, more or less, tell what type of music a band plays based on the album cover art. Zieleniak belongs on a record cover. It is a great setting – the raw, industrial vibe is aesthetically powerful and obvious, without limiting itself to pure aesthetics. It says something about Karol's attitude to 'the system.' Just like the engaged music which he listens to, he wants to go against the rules, he doesn't accept limits (no trespassing at the construction site, no graffiti). To say that Zieleniak was picked for the photo shoot for purely aesthetic reasons isn't accurate. The choice was a statement about values, a manifesto of independence. The carrier of these values is indivisible from its aesthetic form. It is a choice of a certain vibe, which connotes much more than aesthetics and a 'look' – it connotes values. This vibe is his vibe. With his dreads and his t-shirt – it fits him. Aesthetic choices are strongly linked with identity creation processes. The boundary between what's an aesthetic choice, and what's an ethical one, becomes blurred and impossible to define.

Style is important. We do not perceive it as a manifestation of vanity or an attempt to show off. Style is not just what we'd call "being nicely dressed," or furnishing one's room with attention to aesthetic details. Karol has a very clear style, through which he communicates with the world.

Style is focused on being looked at by others. This helps it be understood as a means of communicating with the environment. What I do, and how I act, where I go and how I dress, what foods I eat, which bars I recommend, the nickname I use, and how I decorate my walls, it not only represent my style or taste, it also announce my position in the world. Aesthetic taste is a unique type of screening. It is the basis for choices that a reflexive person must constantly make. It allows us to place ourselves in the world, to find our place. An outfit or a haircut is not an empty act – it is not just aping fashion trends – it is the assumption of a certain place within social structures and relations.

Let's look at another room. Błażej, a Formula 1 and computer games fan, who likes to shoot pool with his buddies. His room is clean and tidy. A bed, bookcase, computer desk with a video game steering wheel. Violet walls. On the walls, a collection of colorful U.S. license plates purchased on Allegro (Polish online auction site). Next to it, a black poster advertising Jack Daniel's. On the bookcase, alcohol bottles with an opened Jack Daniel's. That bottle was a gift for his recent eighteenth birthday party. The researcher working with Błażej described the room as having an American bar aesthetic. This is an aesthetic choice important from a pop-culture standpoint, the aesthetic codes such as the distinctive

'Washington' license plate with a snow-covered blue mountain or a red rising sun above the word 'Nebraska' on another one, carry more meaning than decorating the room with a multi-colored 'something.' Their choice was not accidental.

Similarly, Marianna's various choices are also not accidental. She rides a 'city bike' and got a basket for it for her eighteenth birthday from her friends. In her room, there's a bonsai tree she wanted for a long time – also a birthday present. Marianna has straight blonde hair, which she parts in the middle. She wears the season's fashionable pants: baggy at the waist, narrowing toward the ankle, with a low crotch. For her birthday, she also got a hanger – the symbol of her nascent interest in fashion. She wouldn't call herself a fashion blogger/stylist but has done one session...so far. She tastefully picks out clothes and accessories. She can arrange a photograph: carefully matching the details, finding the right pose and creating a good composition in an appropriate scenery. Marianna is a vegetarian. Sometimes she signs off with a Japanese pseudonym 'Mizuki.' When we ask her for restaurant recommendations she sends us to a Chinese tea house, where a cinematic semidarkness envelopes an aquarium with exotic red fish and stylized oriental graphics. The menu features a choice of teas – green, red, jasmine, pu-erh as well as shrimp dumplings. Who is Marianna? It can be seen in these fragments: how she dresses, her sensitivity, what she listens to, what she eats, how she gets around the city. She combines all of these elements into a single style – in this sense the practices are a way of aestheticizing everyday life.

Style is what connects the multiple levels of an individual's existence: values, beliefs, emotions and learning. Aesthetics is no longer limited to its traditional role. Its social strength and vibrancy is evident in the processes referred to as the aestheticizing of the everyday. Aesthetics is no longer limited to just art, it is also part of everyday life. Now, aesthetic valuation applies not only to works of art or the like, but also to the common, prosaic, banal and everyday events.

Style is a way to express oneself, a necessary feature of a reflexive life. Reflexiveness demands making choices and broadcasting them. The stylization of our everyday lives is the manifestation of these choices on the micro-scale of everyday life. We do not need to join a party, grand political gestures are losing their power. An equally strong signal is sent by working on a fireshow, putting dreadlocks in your hair, riding a bike, or, like Marianna and Karol, being vegetarian.

Reflexive travel in the archives of togetherness

New media have the potential of materializing what is called being together. Togetherness, extended by new technologies, is based on traces, not just visual ones, which fix certain gestures on services such as Nasza-klasa, Gadu-Gadu and mobile phone displays. We saw this with groups of friends, where public comments or tagging friends in photos were evidence of attention, we saw this in love and intimacy where posting photos of loved ones were evidence of fondness and love. This is how digital archives are formed: filled with traces of togetherness practices. They are not created intentionally. They are created as a byproduct of the technologies which register information flows. However, their users know that they can always go back to entries from last week, month, or year. **These archives are not just a statistical guest book, but a living entity which can store fondness and update it in real-time. The traces, which are the building blocks of this entity, can be revisited as they are permanent and searchable. Each individual functioning in new media-mediated social networks becomes surrounded by these traces.**

The young people who worked with us are capable of using these electronic traces, left behind by themselves, other users or network members. Following them, we tried to learn about the paths they use in the network – both the social network, and internet network. This demands that they have certain competencies. First, the development of a strategy for moving around this relationship space, second, a familiarity with technology (its capabilities and functions). In saying that they travel through this space reflexively, we do not suggest that they do so in a calculating manner. The reverse, in fact. Based on our field observations, we saw that the young people used this knowledge of the new media social networks in good faith and in a largely kindhearted way. They use it to strengthen bonds and relations, not to avoid responsibility or to promote themselves.

We noticed that togetherness (social networks, friendships and strong intimate contacts) and the development of their passions are the two most important things for the young people we met.

This discovery steers our research toward observing their activity in these areas. At the analytical level, this leads us to conclusions about how communication technologies which allow constant contact, the prolongation of it, and a development of passions and creative work, mark themselves in identity formation process – in the creation of the 'self.'

'The self' in a relationship network

As we can see, an individual's identity is closely tied to technological practices, thus, the processes which shape an individual's identity ('being yourself') are inseparable from the particular technologies (both the technological infrastructure as well as the general logic behind its use).

Let's take a closer look at this phenomenon. The ethnographic material we gathered moves us from traces and materialized network of social contacts, towards what Mark Granovetter (1973) referred to as **the strength of weak ties. In their daily lives, our young collaborators have constant access (either face to face or screen to screen) to large groups of people and relations with them.** Majka has 428 friends on Nasza-klasa. When Paweł Mazurek, one of our field ethnographers, asked her about a randomly selected 'friend's' profile she was flawlessly able to describe each person: *that's a friend from elementary school; that's my sister's high school friend; that's a girl I used to go to kindergarten with and I haven't seen her in a long time.* There is little room in the friend network for fictitious contacts. Young people uniformly say that they do not accept friend requests from strangers – people they do not know. But, in thinking about the consequences of such an attitude, let us think about what it means to know someone in an era of social networks which materialize weak ties in searchable databases of social relations.

Grzesiek once met a girl at a concert. She was cute. He started looking for her on Nasza-klasa. He searched for: Ania, 15-16 years old, from Warsaw. He got 14 pages of profiles. All his friends said that was a lot of profiles and were surprised that he wanted to search all these digital archives. Grzesiek says that searching 14 pages of profiles is no big deal. He had to click on every profile to see the photos. Thanks to the search he now has contact with the girl. Alek, Grzesiek's friend, says that Nasza-klasa is used for checking other people out. This checking out has a specific pattern. Thanks to digitalization, relationship bundles and functioning of individuals in a network take on the characteristics of a data base. We are not dealing here with people but with a digital record, which, based on social conventions, can be read as information about a given person. In this convention, everybody must decide what 'knowing someone' really means. Ania decided that she knew Grzesiek – the boy she briefly met at a concert and who searched her out on Nasza-klasa – so she accepted the contact.

Locating social relations in a digital sphere does not create the danger that young people will heedlessly fall into its depths, but rather it allows them to reflexively navigate their relationships with their environment, in negotiations of social conventions which clarify the meaning of certain gestures and related terms such as: friendship and knowing each other.

Robert. Facebook and politics

Meeting the democratic left alliance (sld) youth activist from Zahaczewo illustrates how networked communications are changing the functioning of hierarchical organizations. Thanks to skillful use of internet communicators and social networks, Robert is able to develop autonomy within a formal party structure.

Robert used Google to get into politics. *When I was 16, I decided that I wanted to do something, to belong somewhere. I knew that I wanted something on the left-side, so I started searching on Google. On the Federation's websites I saw contact information for the leaders of local youth groups, there were also contacts for the national headquarters. So I called and said I wanted to participate, and then it went very quickly. [...] Recently I became the head of the Federation of Young Social Democrats in Zahaczewo. I'm active, because I want to be active, I enjoy it. It is best to participate through an organization, then you have some resources, you act along with more people.*

Robert radiates energy and enthusiasm. He used to run track and field at the University Sports Association (AZS) but running is now just a hobby, he's concentrating on high school graduation exams. He occasionally plays the violin, but now mostly drums and keyboard with both the school orchestra and just jamming with friends for fun. He attended a musical academy and sometimes DJs eighteenth birthday parties. *Many of my friends are having eighteenth birthday parties so there are a lot of gigs, what matters is how well you play.* During summer vacation he worked, selling clothes at a market, woke up at dawn, then a 50 kilometer commute. He loves watching movies (downloaded from the internet because it is faster and easier), devours books (mostly books which expand his knowledge, describe reality, for example recently about the roots of hate in post-Communist countries which described the events in Kosovo, Ossetia. *I like to read a book in one day, sometimes I read for eight hours straight, either to the end or at least, halfway.* He does not like reading chapter by chapter like a soap opera.)

Robert has a knack for making, maintaining and using these connections. His mobile phone has over 400 contacts, categorized: media, politics, school, family, friends and others. He doesn't always write down names, sometimes he uses a key word. *I wrote your number down as "research project." Even if you call in two years, I'll immediately know who you are.*

Combining social ease with a careful recording of newly made connections, Robert can mobilise the power of weak ties (Granovetter, 1973). His social relationships are also an asset he can use in planning his actions. Contacts collected in his cellphone, on Nasza-klasa and on Facebook become 'social capital,' which he uses adroitly.

One time, I was DJ'ing at a fancy party: catering, security and so on. One of the security guards came up to me to say that he liked the music. We spoke for a bit, exchanged numbers, later on I dropped off a CD of our music. And that was it. Half a year later, when our youth federation was putting together an event, we needed security, so I called him up. It turned out to be a lot cheaper than through a company. You never know when a number will turn out to be important.

Zahaczewo, with a population of 20,000, is the center of Robert's activities. He's interested in national politics but has no personal ambitions about it. *I'm active at the county level.*

I got them on Facebook, so we talk

When the Central Anti-Corruption Bureau (CBA) arrested Mirosław Garlicki, head of Cardiac Surgery at Warsaw's Ministry of the Interior Hospital on February 12, 2007, accusing him of corruption and murder, Robert paid close attention to the story. The then justice minister, Zbigniew Ziobro, announced on television that "No one else will lose their life because of this man." Robert became interested in the low number of transplant surgeries in Poland. *When there was a transplant crisis we distributed organ donor cards during the harvest festival. We gave away about 350 of these cards.*

Robert's main opportunities for getting beyond his local area are congresses and meetings where he can brush up against bigger-scale politics while meeting (and adding to his contacts) people from different regions. *I'm a person who always talks a lot, I'll say hello to anybody, I'm everywhere. After every regional or national congress, I always laugh because that's another 50 new contacts for me.*

Official meetings are dominated by official events which do not leave a lot of time for informal discussions, which is where one can learn the most significant information. When you're talking informally, you can speak more freely. In formal meetings it's sometimes better not to say something, you got to bite your tongue sometimes, before saying something. As soon as you're done catching up and exchanging news its time to say goodbye and see you at the next meeting.

This is why Robert's youth group created an official national internet forum. Robert glances at it once in a while but, as he admits, not much goes on there. Just like in politics, when people are careful what they say to the media. The forum is not the place to find out what somebody really thinks. On the national forum, nobody will write that their regional party is falling apart because there are no volunteers, because they'd be exposing themselves to harm. Just like at the congresses, official discussions have an official tone. However, you can no longer restrict informal conversations between young, networked activists from around the country.

Once we became friends online, more open discussions started on Nasza-klasa and especially Facebook. Thanks to this, I get to talk with people from different regions, whom I normally only see during conventions and congresses when you don't really have a chance to talk. Online we get to know each other better, exchange opinions. In private, small forums nobody's afraid to say, for example, that the regional leader is weak. People want to say things but not necessarily on the national forum.

These networks of politically active friends, developing independently from the party's leaders is still a rather new phenomenon. So new, in fact, that the change is clear even from Robert's perspective of two years of activism. *We're no longer in contact just during the conventions*, he notices. *Until recently, when somebody from outside the region would call us, we knew it was a big deal. Now, we can carry on these informal discussions online in a trusting environment co-created through the social networks' communication architecture.* Politics through Nasza-klasa or Facebook introduces a non-hierarchical, network-based aspect into the hierarchical party structures.

Robert has recently started using Facebook. He signed-up during the 2009 International Social Democratic Youth Congress in Hungary. After one of the lectures, the speaker didn't give an email address and said that the best way to contact him was through Facebook. The attendees were asked if they used the service. Everybody's hands went up, except for the Polish delegation. The same day, Robert set up his profile, and the international meeting resulted in international friendships he actively maintains to this day. *I often talk with the girls from Mexico, whom I met at the congress in Hungary, they're very nice. We talk about politics, but also about what's going on. There are also guys from Germany, from Palestine. I got them on Facebook, so we talk.*

Recently, when he was looking for information about the 2008 conflict in South Ossetia, he was not limited to official press reports. He could ask his own online contacts – his mostly local network, can also reach as far away as Georgia.

I recently met a young woman from Georgia, who was also at the congress, but we didn't talk there. I remembered her because she lead one of the workshops I went to. I wanted to talk to someone who lived through that conflict, and so I found her profile on Facebook.

Communication autonomy

Individuals like Robert, active in relatively formal and hierarchical groups, are increasingly using the freedom of communication offered by networked media. This raises the question if, even though these changes have not made a clear impact, the long-term consequences will result in modifications to the organizations' structures. Given these highly networked and communicatively autonomous activists who are no longer limited to only official congresses and publications, or personal contacts with those geographically closest to them, the ability to successfully use hierarchical communication strategies is significantly reduced.

For individuals such as Robert, who organize their communication activities using elastic and scalable network tools (cellphones, Nasza-klasa or Facebook which allow him to be active both at the local harvest festival but also reach Georgia in his search for information), decentralized and hierarchically flattened organizations appear to be much more effective.

A young activist from a small town who remains in touch with political contacts across the country and the world is changing politics from within. In the hands of young politicians, the web allows them to shape their relations largely independently of official structures. And, perhaps, provides more democracy within democracy.

Successfully being yourself

Digital media act like social mirrors reflecting relations, tastes and images of particular groups or individuals. The moment of this "reflection" or "recording" is not a simple act of registering data. Once again, we're dealing here with a performance mechanism: communication, mediated through technologies, togetherness prolonged and intensified by them, developing passions mediated by them all create what we will call successfully being yourself.

This does not mean that the sum of these digital traces creates an individual. But the experience of being yourself, being true to oneself, having your own beliefs, values, real and important relationships (both friendships and romantic), an authentic self-actualization and fulfillment of interests is crucial for the youth. All of these forms of self-realization are connected to media – blogs, Gadu-Gadu, Last.fm and photos.

Our collaborators, indirectly, made it clear that authenticity and 'realness' are highly important – and falseness is the biggest threat to these values. We found it interesting that, in talking about passions, 'authenticity' was a commonly used word, but talking about interpersonal relationships authenticity was defined in the negative – through the criticism of falseness. *You choose and refine your circle of friends, so that when you're with others, everyone can feel like they're being themselves* – explained Błażej. *When you are with friends, its important to be yourself, to be natural, and not to pretend to be someone you're really not, or to try to raise yourself above others, or follow others by changing your interests, or something within you, to get them to like you. You gotta be with people, with whom you can be yourself.* Falseness is an enemy because it leads to pretending that you're someone who you're not. Their lives are about successfully being yourself, not pretending to be yourself.

Digital technologies and the technologies of the self

Being yourself is doable: to make it happen, you need to be able to make use of certain tools. These tools can be new communication technologies which create an environment conducive to "being yourself," but, on the other hand, the "self" seeks a different quality of experiences, for example, a glass of wine by candlelight. **Agata Nowotny** talks with **Małgorzata Jacyno** of The Institute of Sociology at The University of Warsaw about connections between technologies of the self and digital technologies.

Agata Nowotny: In your book about technologies of individualism (Jacyno 2007), you wrote that individualism is a cultural project of existing in the world, in other words, that it is a form of socialization which attaches a strong significance to choices made in the cultural sphere. The thesis about culturization assumes that the cultural sphere provides tools which are used by individuals to construct their identities. The individual is essentially forced to make independent, entirely personal choices regarding their lifestyle. This is why their lifestyle must appear to them to be their own, and their choices, guided by taste or cultural preferences, bolster this authenticity. You also write, following Bourdieu, that lifestyle understood in these terms is also a tool of emancipation. During our fieldwork we met young people whose practices can be described as an active stylization of life. It appears that this stylization may, in fact, play an emancipatory function when contrasted with the institutions on which the youth are dependent: from formal ones such as school to informal ones like family. Being together, being authentic, are especially important for this age group, and are found among friends, in their 'cliques,' and in intimate personal relationships.

Being yourself, even though largely adapted into everyday conversations, is a technology of the self (Foucault 2000). In other words, in order to be yourself, you have to methodically realize certain assumptions and carry out specific actions. Various technologies help in this – in a more, or less, literal sense. Observing new media technologies, we noticed that they are entwined in the projects of governing oneself and creating a personal identity.

Technologies boost life's reflexivity. They allow classifications, and through classifications they allow one to find their selves, and to align themselves with a certain group – in relation to the whole. That's how it functions with photographs. Visual technologies, digital cameras, editing and cataloguing software and the web infrastructure which distributes them are not technologies which merely neutrally register the world around. A photo not only registers what goes on the world around or captures a moment, but, actually reproduces a social network, classifying who belongs and who does not. People viewing the photos can be divided into the more or less "in the know," which helps verify the degree of closeness and friendship.

Music can function similarly. For young people, it is not only the background of their daily lives but also a serious hobby, which takes up their time and effort. They search out new bands, listen to new songs, trade links with friends and talk about newfound treasures at parties.

We're wondering about the relationship between new, electronic-media based technologies and the technologies of the self.

Małgorzata Jacyno: When we consider individualization as a process of steering individuals toward foresight – both in the economic sphere, and, also in the area of identity. As described by Jean-Claude Kaufmann (2004), new communication technologies are creating a cultural environment in which there is a clear dilemma between the holistic society (nation, class, and especially family) and individuality. There is a strong suggestion that "being yourself," in individualistic terms, can be understood as an attempt to express oneself beyond all determination, or as an effort to reach a certain version of a "pure self." Holistic society proposes categories which are experienced by individuals as absorbing and determining. This is why the "true self" is in conflict with school, with family and with work. New means of communicating can be used for efforts at restoring societal holism. Scientists agree that there are no barriers to their use in various atavistic social projects such as neo-fundamentalism or neo-nationalism. However, I believe that it is no accident that the 'neo' prefix shows up here. Various forms of holism – I'll allow myself to disagree with Kaufmann here – are inspired by the "circle of individuality." Your question does not deal directly with this, so I'll just say that 'atavisms' and communities are functionalized in such a way as to allow individuals to "be themselves." In other words, a holistic society is now becoming unattainable, since it is being called into being to introduce better individualistic practices.

New communication technologies are creating a friendly environment for "being yourself." But, I tend to agree with those authors who see these opportunities as an intensification of certain processes (and thus a good area for study) and not, as entirely new processes (Slavoj Žižek). The "true self" searches for ways to discover the self or creating the self out of experiential qualities – a glass of wine, a good movie, yoga, a warm bath, listening to music or conversation on the phone. You can clearly see that these experiential qualities are incommensurable, which, in turn, means that it is difficult to sum them up to form a coherent whole in which an individual could experience themselves. Second, they lack a certain texture, weight, or density: there's nothing wrong with going from a phone conversation to listening to music. In other words, experiential qualities poorly, if at all, 'enclose' an identity. One phone conversation, immediately demands another. We can call these experiential qualities, after Kaufmann, "small packages" which are constantly being torn. I would refer to them as 'disposable' or 'single-use' packages – products with a short shelf life. The just constructed identity, at the very moment it could be used to enclose an identity, falls apart almost immediately. We can also say that the process of creating such an individualistic identity based on "being yourself" is accomplished simultaneously with the processes of its consumption or exhaustion. For this reason, individuals seek to give these 'single-use packages' some sort of a material form – be it a photo, blog, conversation or recording. 'Being yourself' is possible in a zone lacking societal gravity, but such an environment for identity development efforts cause these experiences (either lined up alongside each other or one on top of another) remain separate with nothing binding them together. In fact, these experiences flee from each other.

However, I would add another point to this interpretation of Kaufmann's arguments. An observation of the **efforts related to mastering the fleeting forms of "being yourself." It appears that we can speak of a certain direction being given to these efforts associated with "being yourself." Thanks to new means of communication, friends and acquaintances can be carefully collected, counted and registered. These relationships, of varying stability and obligational levels, seem to form something similar to the skin tissue or nerve endings of the circle of individuality**, in light of the lack of texture of experience. Sometimes we use the expression: 'external family.' Of course, we should analyze whether we are dealing with a structure that is homologous to that of the family. The individualization of the biographical dimension of a certain individual, necessarily causes the decline of family relationships. Bad relations between kids and parents are perfect evidence of everything going according to "plan," as individualization means freeing oneself from parents. As a point of reference: during the Middle Ages entire families slept in the same bed. All guests, invited or not, also spend their nights in the same room. These days, we often hear teenagers complain that their parents do not knock on their doors before walking in, or, even if they do knock, they do not wait to be let in.

Individualization is a slow process, not without temporary setbacks, however, it mercilessly and constantly is tearing at bonds which we consider to be made of steel. New communication technologies are bolstering this tearing apart from families, as they allow a person to emotionally move out without leaving the physical space of the family home. This is why today we see such strenuous efforts of various social services to restore family bonds. Public service announcements constantly encourage parents to read to their children and to protect them from violence on the internet. In my opinion, it is not at all important what content a child or a young person finds, whom they meet online or if they become either the victims or perpetrators of violence. These commercials can be seen as appeals to try to reestablish bonds which, at the same time, are being torn apart by other discourses. These appeals are meant to motivate parents to engage themselves in efforts meant to stem the tide that is made up of individualizing processes through ineffective means like restrictions, temporary bans, rationing and recording of children's efforts to emotionally move out to their external families.

The answer to the question if these efforts to create a new "nerve system" for the circle of individuality can be referred to as an "external family," must come from different research material – convincing due to its heterogenous nature which shows that different actions and cultural texts are driven by the same motive. The myth, of the cohesive, "traditional" family remains in European culture. In cultural representations, exotic societies or the culturally proximate Mafia, are all based on family structures. The "external family" appears to be an appropriate name for the new media-created environment which is conducive to "being yourself." In today's pop culture we see two types of representations of the family: first, is the family which makes determinations through harming individuals, and, second is the idealized "external family" made up of friends.

The conviction that new communication means simplify and intensify acts of communication is a truth, a truism and mostly a tautology. However, this does not eliminate the fact that some people spend half a day waiting for a message or a contact, and their wait does not necessarily have a happy ending. And, not only because they may not receive a message, receive bad news in the message, or hear from the wrong person. I agree with Kaufmann, that alongside the almost unimaginable freedom presented by the new technologies is an emptiness (hollowness). The "true self" finds and exhausts itself in experientiality: both specific and abstract. We're dealing with experiences felt by an individual in a particular situation: warmth, freedom, concern or wonder at a piece of music. "Single-use" identity packages require some form of permanence and materialization. **New means of communication not only encourage the narrativization of the self – understood to be the search for an appropriate, "enclosing" narrative, but also encourage the narrativization of the self – understood as the recording of the waves of experiences flowing through an individual. The narrative of the 'self' point by point, from one moment to another: the bus splashed me, my head hurts, today I saw X, I spoke with Y, I do not want to go home, because there's gonna be an argument, because I do not take the dog for walks.** These dense, intimate confessions prove the "flammability" of the identity packages. We can also say that "being yourself" has always lacked the coordinates which would place the moment of experiencing into a symbolic reality. Because, as I've written earlier, identity packages are connected to the 'circle of individuality' and they rise and fall apart almost simultaneously, they demand an accounting, a daily report from one's own life prepared for a particular or potential witness who'd be able to confirm that they occurred at all.

There are three conclusions.

New technologies encourage the development of a new life model, which must be described as being a private-public life. The public dimension of these areas is used to build "islands of privacy" – the "external family" or the accounting of the adventures associated with the search for and creation of identity packages. These technologies significantly bolster, and at the very least, create a sphere which supports a tendency associated with the institutionalizing an individual as the "internal world."

New technologies create an environment of developing and increasing the democratization of an individual. Perhaps the democratization of the private world has larger implications than the democratization of the public sphere. The democratization of the private world is part of what Ulrich Beck calls the "secondary" naturalization of the world. The democratization of the public sphere happened "simply" by affording rights to "minorities." The democratization of the private occurs through reflexivisation. I would posit that the uncontrolled reflexivity is connected to the "secondary" naturalization of the world. I do not mean "the ever-present risk." I would rather argue that it is the individuals' need to maintain constant vigilance, a readiness to experiment, to raise self-awareness and so on. The appeals made by "social services" and individual efforts at harmony and internal peace can only confirm that we are in a unique state. "Clear" or "true" "self" is currently the highest level of self-reflexiveness available to an individual.

New communication technologies make clear and highlight the contradiction or dilemma we spoke about at the beginning. The efforts to reach the "true" or "clear" self beyond all determinations are accompanied by drastic returns and escapes toward the old holism and efforts at building new holism ("the external family") confirming the materiality of existence and the dependence on others.

Małgorzata Jacyno

Reflexively being yourself among others

As we've seen, the technologies we are describing, mediate being together and being yourself. In this sense they are a part of developing our identities. The young use them to find themselves and mark their place in the world. This way, they become the subjects of their own management, planning, selection and creation.

A reflexivity aimed at bonds, which is the basis for successfully navigating in the web of social relations, helps an individual map out both their proximate and further surroundings. In the process of mediation a number of changes is occurring, which are themselves subject to reflection by the young. A circle of friends becomes a searchable database. Friendly gestures and innocent glances are materialized into interpretable traces. This new environment demands a rethinking of actions. Because it is a constant process of creation, the rules are continuously emerging and subject to community negotiation.

New technologies are being observed by young people, their negotiated practices and codes of behavior are constantly reflexively transformed. They are not passive objects subject to the operations of technologies.

Searching for proof of one's existence

We get excited by never before seen behaviors which can be observed on the internet. However, their social consequences are largely dependent on the types of new content which appears in the process of communicating. These are not the products of new communication tools, but rather, develop from within relations which people enter into with each other – writes **Mirosława Marody** from the Institute of Sociology at the University of Warsaw, in a conversation with **Mateusz Halawa**.

Mateusz Halawa: While working on this ethnography of the digital world, we met young people for whom networked communication technologies were a natural occurrence. They had various levels of skill in using them, but all of them used digital media, in which content is dematerialized, easily compressed, readily available in quantities unimaginable to previous generations and copied with no effort. At the same time, we saw how networked technologies like mobile phones, internet communicators, and services like Nasza-klasa are changing the understanding of the self and togetherness. There's more reflexivity (providing constant feedback to yourself and the world is built into the architecture of these interactive communication technologies), and there's more intensity (the physical dimension is augmented by digital transfers of content, news, and emotions which are almost always available through these portable gadgets).

The more we talked about this world while preparing this report, the more our questions focused on one of the basic issues in sociology: the question of the individual. We were intrigued how these technologies contribute to creating the "self," which, while experience by each one of us as unique and one of a kind, yet we questioned – d, is this a particular form of socialization unique to the modern era?

Mirosława Marody: That's a very general question, so I will allow myself to break it up into at least two parts: first, dealing with only the "self," and, second, pertaining to the influence of new technologies in its creation. The basic thesis regarding modernity deals with a progressive individualization. Our society is supposed to be made up of individuals, with everyone considering themselves to be unique and special, and even if one doesn't have this experience, he compulsively seeks to distinguish himself in any way possible, even if it is just through a message on his t-shirt. Please notice that this is a claim which combines both descriptive and normative aspects, and so far as we can agree that modern culture imposes a strong normative push toward individualization, the step linking it to the claim that society has become individualized raises serious doubts. I can not even imagine what that could mean, beyond some version of the Hobbesian vision of a collection of independently functioning individuals, fighting with each other for social acclaim. In this vision, even if these individuals enter into some relations, they are strictly on the basis of situationally driven pacts. But we just need to take a look around, to notice that it is a vision that does not correspond at all to reality – both the experienced and objectivized one. **Our involvement in relationships with others not only does not disappear, it actually undergoes an intensification due to, among others, new communication technologies which allow the maintenance of relationships with people, who in other circumstances would disappear from our lives** (vide Nasza-klasa) or would never appear in it (vide Facebook).

Also, it is not as if the feeling of uniqueness of oneself is something specific just to the modern era. In psychological terms, no matter how far back in time we move, individuals always had a feeling of their separateness and uniqueness, they were always recognized by their peers as unique beings endowed with specific qualities. If something differentiated them from today's individuals, it was the fact that in addition to a distinctive "self" they also had a strong sense of belonging to a certain "Us." This, "Us" may have been a clan, family, social caste, class, or nation. This sense of belonging to a common "Us" was not only a fulfillment of their "self," but also a basic guidepost determining the "self's" actions in the social sphere, through the imposition of certain duties.

Thus, we can say that the distinguishing quality of modernity is not so much the establishment of a separate "self," but rather, the disappearance of all these social constructs, which until recently, determined the sense of "Us" – of family, work environment, class or nation. Of course, in the strictly formal sense, these bonds continue to exist, but due to the transformations they underwent, they lost their power to "bind" individuals and impose on them clearly delineated responsibilities. Contrary to Ulrich Beck's famous claim that individuals freed themselves from the binds of social forms, these forms fell apart, leaving a lonely individual on the field of battle.

Mateusz Halawa: But it not that the same as saying that the individual must determine their own 'self'? Regardless of the causes, is not the effect the same?

Mirosława Marody: No, not entirely. The claim that individuals are "freeing themselves" from the bonds of social forms, suggest that they are able to survive without them, that they are able to form their "self" independently, without the participation of others or of society as some higher-level entity. This is the extreme form of the individualization thesis, which has been shaped with significant input from popular culture, which constantly highlights the importance of personal choices, providing behavioral, experiential and personal forms among which these choice should be made. From birth, an individual is faced with a huge and constantly growing supply of these forms and models, and from birth they are exposed to various forms of one message: "You can be anything you want, it's up to you who you'll be." In this context, an individual's life is similar to wondering around in an enormous supermarket, selecting items from the shelves based on personal taste and needs – the elements of forming the individual "self." This explains the popularity of this metaphor among writers attempting to describe modernity.

However, such an interpretation of the individualization thesis is entirely at odds with scientific findings, which unanimously conclude that the process of creating the "self" has a social character, is the result of complex relations which we enter into with other people. In the process of forming the "self," these others appear in two forms. First, it is thanks to them and their specific reactions to our actions during the period of primary socialization that we learn "how the world is, and how I am." It is then that we acquire the belief that we are unique and one of a kind, and that our desires are important; or the reverse – the conviction that even though we are different, we are to some extent just like others, that along with them we are part of a larger whole. For example, as part of a family, a wealthy or poor, or working-class, or Protestant. It is also then that we develop the basic means of dealing with others, we learn conflict resolution strategies, dealing with emotions, openness or shyness and so on. In the transformation of a child's relations with its environment, driven by the changing form of it (partnership, with few children) and new strategies of raising kids, we can find one of the two primary meanings of the theory that individualization is the preferred form of socialization in a modern society.

The essentiality of such a socialization process is not questioned by anybody today, but, I believe, that it is viewed as less important than what happens next. Because once I have this feeling of uniqueness and one of a kindness, it is hard form me to accept that others can affect my activities. After all, it is I who chooses, decides who I want to be, I am the one fighting for my independence. Especially since the subjective observations of the life experienced, are bolstered by social scientists' analyses, which describe, the freeing of an individual from the bonds of social forms, suggesting the need to work on oneself, and underlining an individual's responsibility to himself for the shape of their "self."

Mateusz Halawa: But aren't these analyses and descriptions appropriate to the situation, in which a modern individual finds themselves. Doesn't individualization as a form of socialization force us to act in this way?

Mirosława Marody: They overlook one, extremely significant element, this individualized person does not exist in a vacuum, their actions are inextricably tied to the actions of others, their choices lead to reactions by these others, reactions which can reinforce or devastate our "self." So, yes, I am the one that makes choices, but I do so adjusting them to others behaviors and attempting to avoid causing reactions which would damage my ego. This means that we're dealing with a continuous process of selection of an individual's actions, with the appearance of a certain regularity, in other words, with the process of socialization in the second, non-socialization understanding of the word.

Here we can move on to the second part of your question, the one dealing with the role of new technologies in these processes. The appearance of a new, never-before seen tool always opens new avenues of action. In the case of a development as revolutionary as information technologies, these new abilities include a rapid access to information, the acceleration of social communications, the transformation of time and a certain "disappearance" of space, as well as many other things which are typically analyzed under the heading of "networked society." However, if we take a look at these new technologies from the perspective of their use by individuals, it is striking that they are also used, or maybe even primarily used, to supplement various deficits which arose with the appearance of the post-modern "individualized society." For example, a deficit of unambiguous value judgements connected to the collapse of integrated social communities. In a situation where neighbors in a residential tower mostly do not know each other, where clothing "codes" lost their significance to the uninitiated, where my value at my workplace is dependent on the say so of yet another management consultant and the like, my friends on Nasza-klasa may appear to be the only stable social group which can be used to evaluate my achievements. Also, the deficit of certain, unquestioned truths – we are confronted with various diagnoses and advice from assorted experts and so, in turn, we ask those who've faced or are facing the same problem. Their 'collective intelligence' helps us make our own individual choices. Or, finally, the deficit of community – Facebook or blog audiences form an ersatz closeness, which does not entail excessive obligations which would threaten our independence.

This supplementing of post-modernist social deficits is also happening in less direct ways. Observing the flood of autobiographies on the internet, I sometimes conclude that this eruption of a particular narcissism can only be explained as the search for proof of one's own existence. "Here am I," the authors scream, "please notice me, notice how funny, handsome, athletic and cool I am."

Before the internet and computer era, during my walks in a nearbt park, I kept noticing a woman of certain age, who would come alone, spread out a blanket and strip down to her bathing suit. She would then do some simple exercises with the main purpose of showing off her body.

She had a good figure, and the people strolling by were probably the only ones in her life who were able to see it. She needed these chance glances in order to objectivize what, in her mind, was an important element of her self-image. When I see pictures on photographic portals online, I am reminded of this unknown, lonely woman.

Loneliness is a constant partner of the processes of individualization. A special type of loneliness, "the lonely crowd" as David Riesman described it years ago. In a crowd of separate individuals incapable of forming deeper emotions bonds (a by-product of modern socialization processes) which are too engaging, too full of obligations, and, most importantly, threatening to our 'self,' which, of course, must be unique and only ours. Paradoxically, this 'self' must also be confirmed in relations with others in order for us to believe in it. In this context, the internet becomes a brilliant tool, helping to perfectly balance the desire for independence with the desire for a social confirmation of the individual 'self.'

Mateusz Halawa: But, in addition to filling in these deficits, isn't something new also being created, some new forms of socialization?

Mirosława Marody: I think that it is too early to provide a sensible answer to this question. I believe that it is potentially, such a strong tool, that something like that will eventually come about. But all revolutionary technological changes, in their early stages, were mostly used as tools to meet needs which developed under the influence of a formation, to the evolution of which they eventually contributed. This was particularly clear in the case of printing. It is accepted today, that the invention of printing helped form modern nations, a civic society, the nation-state, and the very experience of a person as an individualized being. But, in its early days, it was mostly used to spread religious texts, which made up the bonds of traditional society. Observing these early uses of print technology, it would be hard to imagine its future consequences for the world.

Things are similar with information technology. We're clearly excited about new, and unseen before behaviors, which we can notice on the internet, but their **social** consequences are largely dependent on the types of content which will arise in communication. These are not the results of new communication technologies, but form as part of relations that people enter into with one another.

Mirosława Marody

SHARING

Everyday life with new media involves constant sharing of music and films as well as sending links to 'interesting' places on the internet. This is the way that groups of users create their own paths on the internet and socialize the experiences and opinions connected to networked culture. Out of these processes of exchanging and sharing, a communalized internet emerges: a familiar, local, cooperatively built web. In this chapter we propose a model of cultural circulation which shows how identity-related practices of finding and sharing are actually multiplying, spreading and creating local audiences for cultural content.

While preparing this report we were struck by **how common the sharing of assorted content and cultural products was**. For the young people of Ziemielin the situation is obvious: if you need something, and you can not find it, you always know who to turn to for help. *Młody* always finds the coolest photos on the web, everybody knows that he's good at it. *When I'm talking about the better websites, I'm talking about all those links that Młody always sends along, he really knows that stuff* – explains Alek. He himself knows a lot about movies, and has a fast internet connection and knows how to download movies. Many of his friends do not even try to download movies themselves because they know that something that could take the whole night to download at their homes, will take 30 minutes at most at Alek's. Instead of waiting, they just ask him for it. Besides, its very likely that he already has the movie on his computer, as he's not only the best "downloader" but also the person responsible for movies in his social circle. That's why he gets them not only from the internet, but also from friends who want to say thanks for other downloads. However, if you do not need a movie, but rather the Photoshop suite – Marcin's your man. He specializes in downloading software. In this fashion, the young people informally exchange services, and these exchanges lead to a fuller life. Together, they can do more.

Our young collaborators trade links to cool websites, send each other photos, show each other the world. Krzysiek along with his buddies sends Gadu-Gadu messages with links to movies that are funny to them, and nobody else. Krzysiek collects these links on his YouTube profile, adding them to his favorites. This way, he always has quick access to them. He has got a sizable archive. He finds them randomly while wondering around the internet. *When something's funny you send it along to other people, if its not, you click on the next video and you look for something funny* – Alek explains. And that's how it goes. This sharing is not only about pooling competencies – having a friend do something that I can not do myself. It is mostly about maintaining relations by sending links and sharing content.

They share music, links and photos. In Zahaczewo online photo sharing services are not very popular. But pictures make their rounds among friends. Most often they are stored on high capacity pendrives. One person puts their photos on it and starts passing it around. The photos travel from person to person. **Contrary to the logic of an analog world – in the digital world content does not disappear at every one of these stops – in fact, it grows.** Usually, someone who takes the files from the pendrive adds something of their own, a bit as a thank-you gesture, a bit to show their friends his own photos or other new discoveries. The memory stick returns to its owner filled with new images and music. **Each day, everyone has more and more megabytes.**

Sharing music is important for Gośka. Music is her passion, and sharing it is an inseparable part in her music consumption. She doesn't have a favorite genre of music or artist. Her enthusiasm for this hobby involves searching out interesting songs by unknown bands on the internet. Last.fm helps with this (see more about

Last.fm on p. 119). Every new find makes her happy. She pays attention when listening in her free time, a precious commodity in her busy days of school and other activities. You need to concentrate and focus while listening to a new track. She only plays well-known pieces as background music while studying or cleaning up. She sends music files to her boyfriend, a vocalist in a punk-rock band, and to her roommate. She likes sharing music, an intimate experience for her, with those who are closest to her. *Most of the links to music, I send to Piotrek and Kaśka with whom I live* – Gośka says. Regardless if the sharing occurs in a larger or smaller circle, it is nearly mandatory. As Gośka explains: *Its kinda sick, but you just gotta share it with someone!*

While observing these young people we couldn't help but think that sharing is an integral element of processing and consuming cultural content. It appeared that an inability to share their findings or treasures with those closest to them, made the entire cultural experience incomplete. Content is shared among groups of friends, as well as those closest. Sharing plays an important role in intimate relationships (which we described more broadly in the "Love" section). Sharing is not a cold flow of data, but a set of practices which are full of heat: they are exciting, important, intense and help forge bonds. The economics of sharing and sending links becomes overgrown with emotions, it is full of warm feelings. In the world we got to know through our young partners there is no division between 'cold' technologies and ''hot' physical space: **this circulation is ruled both by the laws of digital economy, which dematerializes "culture" and transforms it into easily copied and cheaply sent data, and also by the laws of moral economics, which encourages sharing. Only by simultaneously looking at the technological and moral structures of the web, can we begin to understand the new techno-social environment in which cultural content exists.**

According to both our collaborators and web architecture, a film or music file is meant to be passed along, commented and tagged. They want to keep sending it on. In this sense, the cultural practices of the young are, at the same time, the practices of **metaculture** (the personalizing and appropriating parts of various cultural content for their own benefit is largely dependent on its redistribution, commenting, and tagging). Metaculture materializes itself in motion (Urban, 2001), and the circulation process sometimes causes the elimination of differences between content (it is increasingly rare for it to be autonomous) and the attached information that is added by the friend who send along a link, or gives us the file. The comments become part of the content, and the content is, more than ever before, an element of the communication process. Culture is thus expanding in terms of quality (because, texts come with newly built-in meta-texts), but also in terms of quantity (there is more and more of it, and it is this excess, and not scarcity, that becomes problematic).

Sharing results in the communalization of cultural content, which, in turn, enters into the community's pooled resources. In a sense, we can treat it as an answer to the ease of internet access, which is an inexhaustible cultural database. Cultural content, which surrounds and is co-created by this study's participants, is largely non-materialized. Thanks to its digital form, it is easily copied and very portable. Because it circulates through these networks and is constantly in motion, the sharing of it becomes easier, faster and adds to the increased intensity of contacts. Sending becomes a basic modality of the social use of new media, and 'forward it along' is one of the key rules.

Sharing addresses the problem of the wealth and diversity of fragmented materials available online. The existence of multiple sources (channels) carries the risk that everyone will only see and listen to movies and music they are already familiar with, which may remain unknown to those closest to them. A great deal of the practices we are describing is connected to avoiding this risk of fragmentation. **Internet practices largely involve the communalization of cultural content (forwarding it on, sharing through pendrives, burning CDs), sharing experiences associated with it (for example: group viewing or the knowledge that others are also viewing it), appropriating content (the film accompanying this report shows a group of young people recording and posting on YouTube a movies which is a pastiche of their favorite flash-animation) and discussing opinions (the informal opinion marketplace about what is "cool" and "not cool").**

Thus, it is not surprising that some experiences relating to the Web were strikingly similar – but on a smaller scale – to the shared experiences provided by the television. It is an example of the TVfied internet – while the global internet contains infinite amounts of content, the group's version of it is scaled to their purposes and contains content that is known to all of the crew, each one of whom communalizes their choices from the internet's database, creating a cohesive narrative (we discuss the database vs. narration as two competing cultural forms on p. 167). In Zahaczewo, one clique is very familiar with Wykop.pl (a web portal similiar to Digg.com) – they visit it frequently and share links. Their acquaintances who hang out with a different crowd, do not know the website – the visit Demotywatory.pl (transl. note: demotivators) and refer to its amusing photos paired with surprising descriptions in their conversations at school. Networked media allow each of these groups to experience togetherness (and, perhaps, feelings of separateness from others), because, even though they all use the same internet, their usage practices create two different webs.

Sharing is thus inextricably linked with shared-selection and shared-consumption of cultural content. From this perspective, today's young people act somewhat like their parents and grandparents who watched together (not always in the same physical space) a set of their favorite television shows. The architecture of today's communication technologies means that it is no longer enough to sit down in front of the TV at a given hour. A new song must be sent along to the trusted core of friends, and then jointly commented. (This, in turn, requires membership in the right network of friends, at the right time.) It is also an element of negotiating the significance of a given find and of the self. This does not mean that one can not make up one's mind individually. This is not to argue against the individual's independence. It appears that we must treat the practices of sharing and exchanging – of the circulation of cultural works – as a whole bundle of phenomena connected to both culture as well as group and individual identity-creation efforts.

C, like co-internet

One of the fundamental challenges in writing about new networked technologies is finding an appropriate vocabulary to express the scaling effect – the way in which a potentially global network is experienced and practiced as a local one – and will also capture the relationships between people and technology in a way which, on one hand will not fall into technological determinism, but will still highlight the fact that people are actors in a field which features a certain technological infrastructure and has a unique agency in shaping relations. This is how we attempted to do so in this report.

When we speak of:

Affordances,

we refer to the use that can be made from a certain technology or architecture of communication, for example an internet service or a mobile phone.

Affordances are also features available in a device or technology, the capabilities that the user is encouraged to take advantage of. Thus, many internet services feature the affordance of adding comments, creating lists of friends or publishing photos. The affordances of mobile phones include: calling, alarms, storing photos, transporting data from place to place.

Given the above, it is hard to treat the internet as a single, stable object which has clearly delineated affordances. As a collection of technologies, applications, communication structures, and websites, the internet is especially susceptible to changes based on socially negotiated and transferred definitions of what it can be used for.

We can even pose the theory that many of the discussions of the internet define it through the description of various, more or less successful, usages. Similarly, practices referred to as "surfing" the internet, are not based on using an established technology, but rather the co-creation of content and relation which, for convenience's sake, are called "the internet."

This approach to digital technologies underlies their fluid nature. It calls attention to the fact that they do not exist beyond their usage practices, which forces us to pose questions about the manner of using the internet. This is why, an important question in analyzing network practices is one about:

Online horizon

or, the assemblage of possible uses of Internet applications a particular person is aware of. HZ becomes apparent both during the process of experiencing and individual discovery of these capabilities, as well as all the uses that the persons can imagine as potential capabilities (imagined, overheard or noticed from others, or presented in media reports).

Błażej from Parna is interested in Formula 1 and claims to gather information about this topic online. After such a declaration, our ethnographer was surprised to hear that, for Błażej, this was limited to reading information on wp.pl (a mainstream Polish portal) – and not much else. This surprise is a good example of the confrontation between people with differing online horizons.

The web is global in terms of affordances but is always local at the level of social practices. These "localities" – online locations which are known, used, and sometimes co-created – can have various scales. As it turns out, for Błażej, the Formula 1 fan, that online horizons is located relatively close by. Even though he knows English well, English-language Formula 1 websites are "invisible" from his point of view, and thus lay beyond the horizon.

Things located beyond the online horizons are hard to imagine, and thus even harder to find. Still, among the imagined options, only some are actually utilized. One of the requirements for utilization are appropriate

Competencies,

which are developed through successful actions and knowledge. The point of reference for discussing competencies is always based on a specific area, and goals that an individual would like to accomplish within it. In the case of the young people that our ethnographers met, we can look at competencies in a whole variety of areas: from the ability to use software in a way which ensures stable function and usage in accordance with needs, through efficient navigation and finding of content in the hypertext to what can be described as emotional intelligence in the area of screen to screen communications.

Thus, we're talking about using Windows in a way that doesn't cause freeze-ups, sees programs open promptly and avoids online viruses, but also, carrying on conversations on Gadu-Gadu so that the interaction appears as authentic and fluid as face to face conversations with the same person.

Sometimes, there are situations in which individuals lack the competencies or other resources (such as time or money) necessary to fully take advantage of the Web's opportunities. Our observations suggest that, often, methods of using the internet do not require the direct use of it, but rather, are a

Mediated use

of the internet. We can thus watch a movie downloaded by a friend, install a program that a neighbor brought in a USB drive, buy our parents something on Allegro or do homework by pasting a photocopy of a printout that a friend brought with them to school. In our report, new media usage is a much larger phenomenon than their (individualized) use, and the description of their usage is also a description of practices in which people are together, help each other or share with each other.

It is a moment when it is particularly obvious that the practices which organize new media usage become more fully understood when we consider the larger, group context of this use. Among a group of friends online horizons become communalized. Associated with it is the tendency to create shared paths on the Web, an actual example of communalizing the local internet – also known as visiting the same websites, using the same applications and thus creating the

Co-internet.

A co-internet is made up of websites and YouTube movies watched by friends, the photo comments posted on friend's blogs or discussing yesterday's Gadu-Gadu conversation at school. It is a cropped but shared and familiar part of the global network, which in the practices of its use always ends up being a local one.

The co-internet is build on content, the assimilation or co-creation of which become (locally, among a group of co-internet users) a shared experience which can be referred to in conversations and is one of the building blocks of group identity. We discuss a co-internet in order to underline the group use aspect of a new medium, as well as the connection between familiarity with the co-internet content and the relationships which are experienced as togetherness by a group of friends or classmates.

The rules of sharing

What we are describing, and what we had the opportunity to observe, is the functioning of new individuals in a new cultural environment. The electronic media which are co-creating this environment are fundamentally altering the terms on which individuals can act – we, in turn, are asking ourselves how do the young use these new technologies in creating their world. We're answering this question by reconstructing the informational and emotional economics of circulation and by showing explorational-emotional frames of experiencing connectedness and online existence. In other words: we do not feel the need to segregate the online and offline practices, but are rather attempting to holistically reconstruct the experiences of our collaborators. In describing sharing, we outline a bundle of practices which is both technological and cultural, and takes place in both the realm of digital data exchange and in the relations of physical proximity and engages participants as varied as a mobile phone, a group of teenagers, telecommunication networks and campfires. These practices engage both the online and offline worlds – both first-hand experiences as well as mediated ones.

Sharing has a set of rules, which provide unity to these new media practices and stabilize the circulation into commonly recognizable internet 'places' or shared experience, for example how a song downloaded by one person becomes the catalyst for having fun at an eighteenth birthday party. We do not want to describe them as rules of exchange which seek to ensure a balance, where the sum of content sent should correspond to the sum of content returned. The people involved in online sharing are not, as economists would term them, 'rational actors.' This new circulation of digital culture is better understood through anthropological tools, the field traditionally concerned with matters like excess, gift and exchange.

Right after members of the Zahaczewo crew greet each other, either at "Zielone" or some other place, they pull their phones out of their pockets. They sit, smoke cigarettes, talk and all of these goings on are witnessed by their mobile phones laying on either a table or a bench. Even if the phones are all mixed together, everyone knows which one belongs to whom. Everybody knows they can use another's phone if the need arises – due to a temporary shortage of cellphone credits. Mobile phones are private and personal but they can be used by a group of trusted friends. This is why everyone is careful that there's no content in them that could offend or hurt another. Messages with potentially dangerous information, having been read, are quickly deleted. This availability is governed by certain rules. First of all, you always assume good faith and actual need. All attempts to snoop around, to look at information intended only for the owner's eyes is out of bounds. What can be looked at, are photos and music. Sometimes, people trade phones with each other for a few days just to experience a different device, after switching their SIM cards. Crucial to these exchanges is a proper understanding of everyone's roles. The person borrowing a phone does not become its owner and can not pass it along further, their function is similar to that of a trustee. The relationship is based on mutual trust.

Communication responsibilities can also be shared in a group. Parts of Agnieszka Strzemińska's report from Zahaczewo read like *The Argonauts of the Western Pacific*. Communication etiquette among teenagers is strictly regulated and connected to moral responsibilities and addresses issues such as when to call, how to call back, how to indicate that one is waiting for a phone call and so on. Depending on where in the social group the "capital of minutes" was located at a time, the responsibility for keeping in touch with everyone shifted to that person. This practice fits with the "old" model of sharing, one based on **scarcity** of resources; it is much different from the "new" model used in sharing digital content, where the problem is an **excess** of information.

All sharing practices, even though viewed by the young people as spontaneous and informal, have their structure and order. They are based on certain rules, the construction of which reveals an astounding complexity. Sharing, even though tied to the principle of reciprocity, does not aim for only a simple balance. It is used to maintain social bonds and functions as the glue of closeness relations. It allows for a broader understanding of the world and a shared experiencing of it.

As we've mentioned earlier, a strong impetus for the intensification of sharing are differences resulting from the fact that **content exchanged by young people** has the form of easily copied computer files. Compared with physical objects – such as mobile phones – which can not be simultaneously lent out and kept, or with spending money – such as lending a phone to a friend so she could make a call or send a message – the non-material sphere is significantly different. A music file which Gośka shares with her boyfriend, remain with her, on her computer (the computer cubbyhole – a storage space for assorted goods, as she calls it). She does not lose use of it, when she shares it. In this sense, there's a chasm between sharing an mp3 file with music, an AVI film, or a JPEG image, and lending a book, a record, a roll of film, or even a photo print. The culture consumed and co-created by our collaborators is one removed from physical objects. Copying and sharing its creations has lead to an unprecedented multiplication of content. For many, it is experienced as a flood or excess which lead to over-saturation and overstimulation.

In the process of sharing by the young, cultural content becomes multiplied. The closer the young people are with each other, the more cultural content gathers between them. The more intense their exchange and publishing (connections), the more each person brings to the supply of new content. **This is how social relations in the networked era result in an excess of content. This excess becomes a problem in itself, which must be addressed in the context of existing in the network.**

In analyzing this process it is important to consider both vectors of the circulation of dematerialized content: movement "from me," as well as "to us." In many instances, sharing is used as negotiation which leads to the communalizing of knowledge, values and beliefs. Despite the popularity of individualistic values, the process of individual identity creation cannot be separated or isolated, it always occurs in relation to someone or something. That, which an individual rejects does not disappear, but forms an important marker of the boundary of what is chosen. The circulation of cultural works which reflects a complex system of preferences and choices regarding identity is so closely related to the process of identity creation, that it is impossible to describe one without referencing the other.

Identities currently being defined by individuals in a networked cultural environment and digital circulation as the fundamental modality of modern culture are simply two sides of the same coin. Sharing is, in essence, the multiplying of content and, effectively, the production of a supply of mutually shared cultural objects, values and content. We cannot understand the logic of modern cultural circulation without looking at identity, which both motivates the making of choices which power this circulation, as well as being the effect of a particular flow of cultural objects. We cannot understand modern identities without understanding the digital and networked infrastructure, within which these identities are created.

This method of understanding the practices connected to the consumption of culture, and the opportunities created by the internet, reverses the typical approach to the topic. It forces us to concentrate more on the Web's potential to, not so much as allow free publishing (as popular discourse surrounding new communication technologies would suggest) but to selectively and dynamically trade Web links. Of course, among our collaborators there were individuals who fulfilled the traditional definition of artists/creators – guitar-playing Grenio or the Ziemielin photographers – for whom the internet is an excellent tool for popularizing their art. However, it is important to maintain a sense of proportion: creating and repurposing still make up a relatively small part of young people's activities. The sharing of content created by others is still dominant.

Content published on the Internet is send-able and transferrable. Links make the rounds from one GG account to another, from one inbox to the next, from one profile to another. They carry information, but also emotions. The sending of a link can be significant, it may be a gesture of bravery (when disclosing a secret), friendship or love. An analogous act of not sending along a link can mean the lack of desire to get to know the other person, lack of interest, fondness or attention. This understanding of sharing links allows us to understand it as actions subject to moral valuation. Links are good (Weinberger, 2008). They carry emotions which build a close, shared world which unites individuals. The architecture of the Web – which provides the technological underpinnings of this trade – is reminiscent of traditional moral architecture.

Co-internet

The conclusions drawn from an ethnography focused on the process of sharing and exchanging suggest that the young people who intensively communicate, create, evaluate, search for and multiply cultural content use the global network in a specific, local fashion. It is a shared and communalizing use, during which people connected with each other in social and emotional relations create and mark the territory of their media existences, which we call the co-internet.

Let's look at its most important properties.

The co-internet is multilayered. It is made up of devices (computers, laptops, modes, printers, scanners), Web applications (browsers, communicators, P2P software), Internet places/institutions (YouTube, Nasza-klasa, Digart, Last.fm, Blogspot), specific content (conversations, blog entries, photos, movies and the related comments), people (the person downloading, the person giving him a hand-written request for a specific movie or song), and so on.

This co-internet is familiar. Its elements are perceived as known (or becoming known), and the methods and purpose of their functioning is described and clarified in countless actions, which, *de facto*, define both the technology and the content that it transmits. Our collaborators and their friends regularly discuss successful usages, new functions and capabilities and their pros and cons, websites (either recently discovered or frequently visited), and interesting, useful, moving or amusing content. In more or less conscious ways, participants in these conversations are also defining – for their purposes – the norms of using the new media (both in a moral sense, as well as the proper technological use). Some of co-internet content comes and goes in a flash, while some gains cult status. Togetherness, as experienced by our collaborators, always involves, to some extent, knowing or getting to know this content.

The co-internet is built together, both through internet communications, as well as face to face contacts. Sending along links on GG, after school conversations (for example, finding a consensus on a specific blog entry), noting down of key phrases in a cell phone (to remember which pages to check at home), the making and publishing of photos from a trip out of town, and then reading comments on them, are only some of the activities which, taken together, resemble the creation of shared paths: some become more and more familiar, others, forgotten, become abandoned.

One of the most important practices of building the co-internet is searching. It is worth noting that searching is an affordance in a great variety of applications and websites, which means that the ability to search something (the internet, a site, a file) becomes obvious and expected. Searching is not always simple. This is why sharing the effects of one's searches can be considered as a gift to co-internet building. For the gift to be successful, one must have something to offer and also know that the recipient would appreciate the item. The question of 'Who do I send this to?' is a common but fundamental one, which helps make the social network more reflexive.

The co-internet has a clear exploratory dimension. If we were to look at this collection of machines, programs, and circulating content, along with the people who create it (by publishing) or help map it (by searching and commenting), we will see a **techno-human search mechanism, whose perpetual labor is based on selecting, filtering, evaluating and gathering assorted content.** In other words, if media remediated relations create a multiplication of content, than this abundance must somehow be managed, sorted and selected. In this sense, the emergence of folksonomy was a necessity resulting from the fact that friendships online inevitably posed a problem of ordering the flood of data brought on by these friendships. A process related to the functioning of this search mechanism is the communalizing of internet horizons of people participating in building the co-internet. The filtering and further resending of content engages social practices and identity-motivated searches, as well as algorithms and interfaces which create the infrastructure of web access.

Co-internet has clear emotional and identity-related components. Both the content coursing through its veins and the rules of its circulation reflect and illustrate the existing web of social relations, while helping create them. The importance of the co-internet stems from the fact that it is built together, and its content is entwined with the manner of experiencing the world, and is viewed and experienced together. The co-internet can be an excellent source for identity definition, as the direct connection between knowledge of its content and a closeness within a group of peers is highly visible. It is also a venue for the intensification of togetherness and mutual sharing.

The process of co-internet creation is a living illustration of one of the main theses of our report: circulation (or the manner in which cultural content travels, multiplies, is created, searched and selected) is closely bound with identity formation processes. In other words, the use of specific affordance offered by new media, is not a question of calculated choice or ease, but rather, bound to social and moral concerns.

GEEKING OUT. PASSIONS IN THE NETWORKED ERA

In this chapter we show how new communication technologies affect practices of creating, learning and sharing of passions, abilities or knowledge – the various geek outs people have. With the web, energy, competencies and ideas are no longer scattered, but can become stronger and more focused. Having a passion in the networked era means taking part in activities whose importance and consequences can far exceed your own input. Whether it involves collecting old photographs, learning everything about a favorite band, or creating photo projects – a networked geek out can mean a faster and more in-depth passion.

We go somewhere, do things, take photos, go for a biker ride somewhere. Each one of us has something we geek out on. Everybody's doing something in their free time and isn't bored. But, Mateusz, on the other hand, if he doesn't have a job – he's just waiting for school to start. He's happy he'll finally have something to do, have someone to joke around with, because he's bored during vacations. That, to me, is the definition of not having real interests: being bored during free time.

Alek

I really got into it, and others are getting into it as well, that's when its worth to keep going with it. Otherwise, what's there to talk about? About what's on TV, or that you got shit-faced this weekend?

Danek

In the previous chapter we showed how reception, creation and transfer of cultural content figures in young people's togetherness. Music, photos and movies encourage the intensification of contacts, help reflexivize friendships, and cement relationships by circulating through techno-human networks. They allow people to get to know each other better, define themselves, and outline being together in a group. To our collaborators, networked passions were a value by themselves, an oasis of freedom for young people restricted by the adult world. They can choose who to spend time with after school and how to spend their free time – time that can be "wasted" or spent pursuing their passions. And, even though the teenagers we met were sometimes bored, they still viewed "doing nothing" as something to be avoided.

Ewa plays guitar. She picked it up from her older sister's boyfriend, who has a few guitars. She looked on when he played, and when she got her own guitar, she started teaching herself from tabs. She never took any guitar lessons. On fan forums of Blink 182, a pop-punk band, she meets up with people in order to play together online. Everybody sits in front of their computer with a guitar and tries to play a song. On Gadu-Gadu they compare tabs found in books or online and pick the best ones. Then she tries to play the song, and if things do not go well she can always go on the forum to ask for help. Either on GG or the forum, Ewa describes her problem and others help her out. (Thread titles on similar forums include: *Tuning a guitar, Hurting fingers, Does being left handed make it harder?, My first guitar – electric or acoustic? Strumming – looking for help*). They write because its easier, and besides Ewa rarely uses Skype's audio connection as it uses up too many of her limited kilobytes.

***Ostry* and his friends practice fire dancing.** It started two years ago. Somebody – nobody really remembers who exactly – showed someone how to twirl chains with burning kerosene-soaked cotton balls at the end. *Ostry* got into it, learned the basic tricks and maneuvers, and then they started to learn on their own. They searched the web – on forums, YouTube, at Kuglarstwo.pl (transl. note: juggling.pl) – to see how it gets done, how to make affordable equipment. On

YouTube there was a film which described the process step by step. You need a kevlar blanket – it burns slowly and well – *Sharp* found one at a firefighting store in Wrocław. Then chains and tennis balls. They have two sets of their own equipment: the worse one for practice, the better for performances. They've gained some fame in town: they fire danced at events at the Zahaczewo Cultural Center and at one wedding. Between performances they practice and exchange links from various shows or meet up to watch films from the web. They learn new shapes – the speeding burning balls create unbelievable patterns – and study the difficult art of smoothly going from one part to the next. On a fire dancing forum *Sharp* found a more advanced group from a neighboring town. He wants to practice with them, maybe even have a common show, because the other group can perform long shows with figures *Ostry* hasn't mastered yet. Practicing with others is the most enjoyable part, you can learn a lot and show others what you can do. *Ostry* had a chance to do so when he was at Przystanek Woodstock (transl. note: Polish youth and music festival) and at the Fine Arts Academy. *Ostry* wants to see more girls fire dancing (they have cat-like movements). They could twirl fans – a type of special burning finger covers. It would look beautiful – especially with live music. He saw one such show in a film he downloaded.

Kamila also does fire dancing, but her biggest passion is theatre. She wrote her first play with her friend Helenka in the third grade of middle school. The play was put on with help from her Polish language teacher during the school's cultural days when comedy shows, spoken word performances and theatrical plays are put on. Unfortunately, in high school her hobby faced a roadblock. Despite getting into the best high school in the area, it didn't have a theatre club. Despite the disappointment, Kamila took things into her own hands. *The theatre club exists because I announced that we'll start and avant-garde artistic group, and now we have one* – she recalls. Kamila receives some support from the school (including financial) but frequently complains that the teachers are too passive. Kamila has a dedicated email account which she uses to receive newsletters from her dream universities, information about theatre contests and festivals. She often looks on websites of dramatic academies and cultural centers in her region to find other opportunities to become involved in the young theatre artist's circle. When she finds information that could be useful to her friends who are interested in photography, painting or poetry she forwards the links to them.

Piotrek and Paweł from Parna play in a band: Termin Przydatności do Spożycia (transl. note: use-by date). Piotrek plays the drums, Paweł the guitar. Band members know each other from elementary school, most live in the same housing development. Their initial connection was the love of RPG games and punk rock. At a concert of their musical idols, the band *Taksa Klimatyczna* encouraged them with the words: *play, anyone can play!* The guys took the advice to heart, but exhibit a good amount of distance to their musical abilities. *We're not musicians, we're just guys who like to play.* They excitedly relate last Saturday's concert: *it was awesome, nobody knew us there, we were a complete surprise, girls were dancing on the tables, the energy was unbelievable!* Their frontman, *Falafel*, is a bit less enthusiastic, complaining that his bandmates are too careless when it comes to practice times they set on Gadu-Gadu, they come late and do not send him text messages about it. They all use the internet to follow other local punk bands' efforts.

Gośka, the girlfriend of *Termin*'s Piotrek, cheers the guys on and is very proud that they sometimes listen to her advice when working on new songs. *(Repeating the chorus was my idea! Really!)*. As she explains, she loves music: *I listen to music everywhere, since I have an iPod, I really take it everywhere, on the way to school, from school, when I'm waiting for someone, whenever I'm not walking with someone. At home, my computer is always on. I've got external speakers that I can hear the music in every room. I listen from the phone when we're in the forest or sitting on a friend's balcony.* Wtyczka from Zahaczewo also loves music. First thing in the morning he turns on his mp3 player which he uses to mark the three minutes he brushes his teeth (one song equals three minutes). Afterwards, he doesn't take out his headphones. Music is one of the most important elements in the lives of our collaborators, it accompanies them from the first moments of the day – as one of the teenagers we spoke with explained. Another of our collaborators, Karol from Ziemielin, after taking part in the day-long no new media experiment, said that he felt strange in the morning on the way to school, when he didn't put on his headphones.

Finding new artists, playing an instrument, theatre, fire dancing and photography are only some of the geek outs which we came in contact with during fieldwork. There are more. Greniu uses the web to help create his music, Janek, along with a group of history buffs he met online, is studying his town's history. Robert, the left-wing party activist, sometimes carries on informal political discussions through Nasza-klasa. Majka, has an online radio show where she shares her love of reggae. We've already met Marianna, the neophyte fashion blogger. Even though the range of their interests in enormous, there was one unifying belief among all the teenagers we met: they were convinced that having a passion for something, or hobby, is extremely important. As Agnieszka Strzemińska wrote in her field study report: Having a passion for a certain activity *is fundamental, because it provides something to talk about. Kamila's classmate Ula is a dancer, she goes to workshops. Kamila respects that, even though the two are not friends. If it wasn't for this hobby, Pola would get lost in the crowd,* she says. A hobby is not only important because of its social cachet. Having a geek out causes a person to become interesting not only to others, but also to herself.

Kamila speaks poorly of people who do not follow their interests and focus only school and fun. She dreams of studying performing arts and sees her future in theatre. Her father is not convinced, encouraging her to pursue banking or bookkeeping. *He wants my life to be focused on making money, and we're unable* to agree on this, as we simply have different opinions. He believes that money is more important than my emotional well-being, and this is why I work. I don't have to work, I'm an only child and both my parents have jobs, but I want to work to show that even though I have somewhat of an artistic soul and want to pursue it and it's important for me, doesn't mean I don't have to make money. I want to show that I can make a living out of my hobby, or at least keep doing it after working hours. This is what I'm trying to prove. I've been working for two years as they don't hire people younger than 16. Her accomplishments in the theatre field are also strong points in her argument with her father, as she's participated in theatre workshops held as far as Warsaw. She's tries not to miss any chances that could help her achieve her theatre dreams. She's assiduously compiling experiences, spends a lot of time at the Zahaczewo Cultural Center, where, along with her boyfriend Bartek, she helps with all the events – from Zahaczewo Days to harvest festivals. They also travel with Bartek's comedy troupe, and they've even performed for the Polish community in Austria.

Having a hobby is not only a valuation criteria for judging peers but also adults. Kamila gets angry talking about her school, where she didn't find anyone who would inspire her theatre activities. She found her master – her "theatre dad" as she calls him – in another school. Kamila considers Mr. Roman to be the ideal teacher: he always has time for the young people and is full of initiative. Kamila works on her plays with him, he supervises the rehearsals which helps keep the actors' in line. Mr. Roman's encouragement is a strong motivation for Kamila, and she appreciates that he believes in her, and tells her she can achieve success in the field. Mr. Roman is proof that interaction with a 'master' is still very important for young people and hard to replace. Which does not mean that it can not be augmented with independent work. Kamila is aware that for her, a small town resident, there are fewer opportunities to achieve success in theatre, especially compared to her peers from large cities. She's trying to balance these differences, and the internet is an invaluable help in that. Newsletters from performing arts schools and websites which discuss young theaters, which we described above, films from semi-professional theater performances (theatrical performances which can be seen on television are so far removed from the young theatre aficionado's reality as to not be helpful) allow her to keep abreast of events from well beyond her region. Thanks to the internet, she's able to easily gain contacts and information that would otherwise be difficult to access in a small town. This is true not only with cultural interests which are supported by established institutions. This is particularly significant as our collaborator's geek outs do not directly follow established canons – they're not concerned whether their interests cover theatre, fire dancing or guitar playing. The intensity of the hobby is what's important for them, these hobbies' hierarchies are fluid and negotiated within groups. The teenagers we met do not generally have 'generational experiences,' but they value particular group experiences of culture (songs rather than bands, films rather than directors or movements, particular games not game genres, particular YouTube clips or specific websites such as Demotywatory.pl) which create their shared and particularized frame of reference (even if only for a short period of time). This type of work is very important – it can be connected to long-term plans for life, as with Kamila or the young photographers from Ziemielin) but it does not have to be. What's important is having fun, gaining satisfaction and a feeling of fulfillment. As *Falafel* told us: *I like our song so much that I can't help but laugh! Sometimes we stop playing just to enjoy it. We're not looking into the future.*

Last.fm: vibes via an algorithm

Music benefits from the digital form: it becomes more portable, is easier to organize, count and label. Gośka and Marta, friends from the same high school, share music and monitor their evolving tastes in real-time.

This generation has postmodernism in its blood, a 30-something, Polish teacher at a respected Warsaw high school told us, after we discussed our project with her. By "postmodernism" she also meant their evolving approach to music. Young people used to be more intensely and authentically involved in music, Katarzyna, the teacher claims. Metalheads only listened to metal, and dressed like metalheads. *At school dances, when types of music changed, there was a full-scale change of people on the dance floor – one group would conspicuously stand against the wall, while the others, who were just standing against the same wall wondering why anyone would dance to the previous song, would begin dancing. Now, everybody dances to everything.* (More about cultural omnivorousness on p. 107.) Their involvement in music is more shallow – Katarzyna suggests – without any obligation, it seems less serious than it used to be. (On the other hand, they can not sit still without music – Katarzyna allows her students to listen to their mp3 players while writing papers in class. They sit with one earbud in. They can listen as long as the music isn't loud enough to disturb others). This poses questions about new ways of living with music. How does music circulate among our collaborators? How do new technologies – with the explosion of easily copied files which can be carried by the thousands in pocket-sized mp3 players, music trading platforms on the internet, fan forums, social networks where people listen and talk about music – affect that paradigm of youth culture that is music. The changes which Katarzyna labelled "postmodernism," are complex and it is hard to say whether we're seeing a less engaged involvement with music, or simply new ways of functioning in a world where countless musical sources are easily available online. Generally, Katarzyna's intuition appears to be correct: there's something going on with the young, new technologies and music. Our collaborators, living in an era of abundance, consume more cultural content than any previous generation. This content is doubtlessly more diverse than ever before. Cultural preferences are still significant points of reference in establishing identity, but the process of constructing the "self" through musical choices – negotiating musical genres, tastes, vibes and subcultures – is becoming more complicated. One way of shedding some light on these changes are the practices used by our collaborators mediated by the Last.fm service.

Musical entanglements

Last.fm is most frequently referred to as a "social music portal," but that does not capture the complex set of practices that make up *being on last*. In the lives of Gośka, Marta, and many other teenagers we met, Last.fm is an online institution. Thinking of an analog world analogy it is a combination of a record store, band badges attached to backpacks, a home record shelf, a radio, a music critic, a more knowledgable friend, a mentor, a band poster, and a cultural events calendar in one. *Last.fm is a music service powered entirely by the listeners* – the website claims. Generally, the portal is based on a user-generated music labeling mechanism powered by keywords (a community-based system in which classifications are not made by one music expert but rather by a community of equal-status users). In other words, an algorithm-powered crowd sourced classification which aids in navigating an extremely broad musical database.

In social contexts, the eternal "what kind of music do you listen to?" question still exists. However, when portable musical collections amount to dozens of gigabytes of music files by hundreds of artists from a broad range of musical genres (as is the case with Gośka and Marta) – the answer becomes highly problematic. Fortunately, the girls, like many of their peers, have a sophisticated tool which can quantify and provide objective answers to the nebulous question of musical taste (and, to some extent, their identities). At any time, they can look up their individual listening statistics for particular periods of time which include recently listened to songs and most frequently listened songs over the last three, six or twelve months.

Music plays a large part in Gośka's life. Her boyfriend Piotrek is the drummer in a punk rock band *Termin Przydatności do Spożycia.* She also devotes a lot of time to music. She loves going to band rehearsals, concerts, discovering new sounds (she speaks disapprovingly of people with *shallow musical tastes*). She especially loves music that mixes genres and listens to music all the time. She hates school tests because they have to be written in silence. At home she listens on the computer, the main stationary music player in her life. *At home, my computer is always on. I've got external speakers that I can hear the music in every room.* Outside of home she listens on the iPod, which is her favorite and most beloved gadget. *My main playlist has Clint Massel, Pearl Jam and David Bowie, the rest changes frequently.*

Monitoring musical tastes

In total, I've got about 40 gigabytes of music, all of it on iTunes [a music player and cataloguing program, which features playlists and transfers songs onto the iPod]. It scans all music files, album covers, it converted everything for me, all by itself! Gośka loves iTunes, mostly because it allows her to easily organize her expansive musical collection. Each file, in addition to music, also contains metadata about the artist, album and track title – thanks to it she can scrobble.

Scrobbling is the automatic transfer of this data from a portable mp3 player or PC onto the Last.fm profile. Thanks to scrobbling, Gośka can follow her personal listening statistics. As she says: *I can see the evolution in my tastes.* Last.fm is able to accurately register her musical tastes which are an important part of building her identity. It registers playbacks in real-time, balancing her musical hyperactivity. *I've got thousands of favorite artists, who change everyday, I can't limit myself to just one. I couldn't even name my top forty! There's no such thing as 'favorite' – that's what Last.fm is for,* adds Marta.

The portal encourages scrobbling, to help the Last.fm community to learn what you listen to. You also get personal rankings, music and concert suggestions, and connections to listeners with similar tastes (musical neighbors). Scrobbling provides information about which tracks you listened to, and by tagging them (adding genre labels) users place the songs in particular musical categories.

This precise individual data powers the "Taste-o-meter" which calculates the level of musical compatibility with friends on the portal and creates lists of users with similar tastes (musical neighbours) based on their listening history. Based on the "people who like this also listen to..." principle, Last.fm suggests other artists. In his analysis of the Last.fm phenomenon, Artur Szarecki referred to this mechanism as a "loose anchoring" or "drifting at the dock" (Szarecki 2009: 356) – through it, users becomes more and more entrenched in their taste or vibe based on all the previous listens, and Last.fm suggests new musical directions that maximize the probability that the suggestions will match the taste (as established by the "Taste-o-meter).

In other words, the user continuously receives new and unknown (and thus exciting) music in their familiar and preferred genre.

Musical searches

For Marta, Last.fm primarily orders and particularizes musical experiences. It also helps develop her musical fascinations. Her first serious musical finds were inspired by her older brother. *He was the one who initially suggested songs to me, he was interested in music, but my brother is more classic rock and I'm from the pop generation.* After catching the music bug, Marta began to look more at her peers, who are most often the guides to music. Michał is Marta's friend and the singer in a punk rock band, he became her next music mentor. She laughs and says: *Michał downloads so much music that if the cops caught him he'd get life in prison.* It started with a close friendship and frequent visits to Michał's house, music was usually playing in the background. *If I really liked something, Michał would either burn me a CD or give it to me on a pendrive. He sent links and I would look into it further – he's an important source for me.*

Many of the high school students we met treat music very seriously. It isn't unobtrusive background noise – music stimulates them, inspires them (for example, the artistic photos on Krzysiek from Ziemielin's blog are often paired with quotes from songs he listens to). All of the researchers participating in the project met people who were immersed in music. Olka Gołdys who worked in Parna wrote about the "**searching avant-garde**": *they have the biggest hunger for music, those most interested in it, those who consume it the fastest, they use the Web efficiently. They download a lot and do it quickly, they shoulder the burden of finding it and passing it on.*

Since Last.fm's suggest a song function entered Marta's life, she occasionally uses it, but does not solely rely on it. She often undertakes solo musical explorations; her inspirations come from many places: you just need to have yours ears and eyes wide open. *Sometimes you hear something interesting sitting at a bar, you just need to remember a part of the lyrics, and then you can find it online.* Individual searches (entanglements of entanglements) and suggestions from friends are too exciting and educational to be abandoned. *I know about music from friends, my own searches and Last.fm*, she explains. However, it seems that Last.fm has permanently entered the musical world of many young people, and is commonly perceived as a *measure of taste*. In fact, it is a unique and innovative type of an algorithmic crowd-sourced authority – the catalyst of choices of thousands of users.

Scrobbling yourself

Last.fm is a social network, but is generally not used to accumulate friends, but to pursue one's musical interests within a selected group. On Last.fm,

Gośka only has 30 friends – much less than she has on Nasza-klasa. *It's sick but you just gotta share music with somebody!* – she says. She's much more careful about picking friends on the portal, as they gain a very detailed look at her musical tastes, which are an important element of her identity.

There are ways to retouch your profile: you can delete unwanted tracks, some people run up their play counter by leaving their Winamp on during the night with an appropriate playlist (this is a Scrobbling variety focused mostly on self-presentation). But, for the most part, scrobbling is a tool of self-discovery (it is important to know what, when and how often one listens), so that by gaming the system you also lie to yourself.

Providing a person with such a window into your musical identity requires trust, and Gośka's trust was once abused. *I had an unpleasant situation when I gave a guy access to everything on my profile too quickly, and he made jokes about the fact I listened to Coma* – since then I more careful. That's why it may be easier to bare all before unknown users of the service, with whom we only share our musical fascinations than with acquaintances whom we do not completely trust.

Apologizing for Britney

By scrobbling, Gośka receives a statistical extract of her musical tastes. But raw numbers do not explain the motives for listening, they leave out emotions and situations which prompt particular songs. The most listened to songs are not necessarily the favorites – sometimes the most emotionally significant songs are listened to in moderation. This is why, despite regularly scrobbling, Gośka claims that *Last.fm doesn't really show what I listen to*.

In his paper on Last.fm, Szarecki notices that users sometimes feel the need to explain the results of their scrobbling or the reason for their deletion from the profile (such information gets posted in the "about me" field). We can find comments such as this one: *I finally deleted my songs, because Britney Spears was disproportionally represented. It's not my fault I own all the remixes of her singles.* The "Taste-o-meter" currently counts the number of listened to tracks (in the future perhaps also the length of playing time), and while it provides a statistically objective description of musical identity it is far from a perfect tool. However, Gośka – despite not being in full agreement with this musical mirror – values the knowledge she gains by scrobbling. Her Last.fm profile brings out her musical statistics, and thus enriches and stimulates her process of self-reflection.

A never ending gallery opening

"My collaborators are crazy – in the best way possible – about being creative," wrote Paulina Jędrzejewska, one of the ethnographers who worked with teens in Ziemielin. "They can not just go to the lake to spend time with each other, swim and sunbathe. Their real 'fun' is taking a camera and shooting photos of friends jumping into the water, telling them to get covered in mud, to squeeze the rolls of fat on their stomachs, or to show their butts." Earlier in this report we looked at the same trip to the lake (p. 62) as an example of how taking photos is a part of togetherness. In this section, we take a look at photos and photography as an example of a geek out: something more than "just" taking photos. (As we saw earlier, the role played by "just" photos is very complex.)

When he goes on a class trip, Krzysiek takes two cameras with him: a portable digital one and a large analog camera. Each one is used differently. The things that separate taking photos from photography are goals, effort, levels of involvement, and often, equipment used. The prosaic taking of photos is less reflexive and more of an automatic and functional activity. It serves a specific purpose, for example, taking a picture with a cell phone to send it to a friend, capturing something interesting discovered by happenstance, recording a funny event or an amusing pose made by friends. These types of snapshots are usually taken with a camera phone as it is usually within reach. Occasionally they get taken using a 'monkey' or a simple digital camera. Photography, on the other hand, involves taking photos whose purpose, while clear, is not functional. Such a photo might contain a photo effect, capturing which requires an adequate mastery of the medium and a high level of competence in using the equipment.

The group of photography enthusiasts from Ziemielin work using the project method. They consciously use the term "project" and think of what they do in professional terms. They budget their time and energy. Krzysiek: I've got an idea for a project and that's what I do, I used to have time when I didn't take photos, which is a shame, because I was wasting my time. A project not only entails clearly marked time limits but also a definite goal. It is a closed entity, which, even at the beginning, has an expected endpoint. Its final stage is publishing the photos in some manner. It could be an actual show at a gallery, but most often it is done on the internet. As Paulina Jędrzejewska described it, the internet is a place where the show opens every night. The projects are varied. Karol's idea for portraits of people wearing Elvis-like gold sunglasses and sideburns – published on his blog is one option, another is Krzysiek's project of photographing people with their dogs. Photos from this series are published on a dedicated blog (one of several that he runs).

However, it is *Młody* whose ideas are clearest. He takes photos everyday, has good equipment and spends a lot of time and effort on his photoblogs. He's seriously considering a career in photography, and like Krzysiek, is considering studying photography in Opava. *Młody* also makes series of photos. He's got many ideas. One of them was photographing giant plastic ice cream cones that line sidewalks in front of stores. He also did a series on tram drivers in front of their street cars. Those photos were later exhibited in the city's trams. He would take the tram to observe people's reactions to his works.

The young photographers we met had all types of digital cameras. There were also some analog ones borrowed from older siblings or bought on Allegro: a 35mm Praktica, a medium format Lubitel. Some even had professional equipment of a certain age from manufacturers like Mamiya and Hasselblad. A better camera provides more options. Mastering its functions requires practice and the development of competencies: [...] *you know when you have such a crappy camera, the options are also limited, afterward I got the SLR, which I kept asking for, and that's when the bigger depth of sharpness came in, and when I got this camera I started doing photo shoots with the girls* – recalls *Wtyczka* from Zahaczew. A new, better camera creates challenges: photography is not just noticing interesting things and creating the right frame, but also the knowledge which diaphragm to set for what exposure time or, with an analog, which film speed to choose. It is also about knowing what effect will be achieved based on these settings, planning it out, considering if the equipment is appropriate. Search for information online, ask friends.

Photo subjects are different for analog and digital cameras. For Krzysiek, the difference is obvious. As Paulina Jędrzejewska, the ethnographer who worked with him wrote: on the trip, he'll take different photos with the analog (a hole in the road, a piece of garbage, a man on the street) than with a digital (photos meant to capture vacation memories, classmates, historic buildings). Digital photos are cheaper, easier, simpler to take, and are thus less valued. This is why digital snapshots are typical souvenir snapshots – meant to capture moments that they'll want to return to.

On the other hand, analog photos are seen as evidence of an ability to combine knowledge, with ability, an artistic vision and creative ideas. They also reflect an old-fashioned sense of "professionalism," a status that some of the young people we met aspire to. By using an old technology (through the internet – a good analog camera is much less expensive than a professional digital one), they invoke the image of a professional photographer, who is skeptical toward technical novelties. At the same time, some of them break out of this pattern, as their skills, despite their young age, are surprisingly close to "professional."

Photography is significant not only to photographers. Another important aspect of the hobby, are informal photo shoots. In the group of young people with whom we worked in Ziemielin, Krzysiek is an expert in organizing such events. He has a blog that has not yet gone live – he's waiting to gather more photos. He puts his photos from the shoots onto the blog. The main theme of the photo shoots are portraits which are stylized to resemble stereotypical characters, whose arrangement is meant to draw a reaction from the viewer: to annoy, provoke, amuse, and challenge preconceived notions. As Agnieszka Strzemińska wrote from Zahaczew, photo sessions are a way of spending one's free time. In Zahaczew, people go to "the green," to see friends who usually hang out there. There is a picnic table and a bench. You can sit there and be bored or do something. They agree to meet up, usually just girls, and they go somewhere 'cool' to think up poses and arrangements. They take photos confidently. They're not afraid, and have complete awareness of this communication medium.

The Zahaczewo photo sessions began when a friend asked *Wtyczka* to take some cool pictures of her for Nasza-klasa. This was before sessions became popular, now, they all agree, they've become a standard activity. Ideas originate from different sources, wrote Agnieszka Strzemińska from Zahaczew: fashion magazines, blogs or own ideas, some are freestyle – they go to a shoot and snap pictures. Then the photos are processed in Photoshop and land on their blogs, the best might be posted on Digart. The young people pose confidently and worry free, but photography really fascinates them. In designing this report we wanted to have photos taken by a professional photographer, Tomek Ratter, as well as ones taken by our collaborators and ethnographers. Tomek's presence among the young people provided us with many observations. He quickly became a favorite among our collaborators, they asked him about his equipment, education, experience. We worried that the appearance of a new person, who would "take photographs" and act as an "expert," would be stressful and create a distance from the teenagers we worked with. In fact, the opposite happened; the world of the young people we met is one where a camera lens builds connections not divisions. Tomek, a 27 year old student at the Opava photography school, was full of enthusiasm for his art – a passion that reminded our participants of their own interest. The day after the photo session, one of our collaborators posted a photo of Tomek. Below we read: *Tomek who shoots these has a nice ass!*

Digart: community of practices, online studio

Publication is the final stage of creating photographs – and the start of the next step in their social existence. Photos differ not only due to formal qualities, the time and place where they are taken but also through the context in which they finally appear online. As long as photos remain on the artist's hard drive, they are part of a private, limited archive – disorganized and un-processed (thousands of photos which do not get deleted but also aren't looked at – computer folders often have some unrotated photos). When they appear online, their status changes. All of the photographers categorize them for their own purposes – it is this categorization which determines the distribution channel. It is significant that even analog photos exist, in effect, as digital ones after the negatives scanned and posted online. The fact that none of the analog photographers we met make prints, is not just a matter of wanting to reduce costs. In the digital media world, each cultural artifact must reflect computer logic – so it must exist as a digital file. This is why, even analog photos need to be scanned to become useful in any way. Photos are in perpetual motion: they are being sent, shared, they draw looks, invoke memories, testify to the photographer's skill or lack thereof. This circulation is their inalienable context, without which they cannot be properly interpreted. Posting a photo on Nasza-klasa is one thing (either into a gallery or as a profile picture), putting it on one of your blogs, another, while posting on Digart a third thing. Among the young photography aficionados, Digart holds a unique position. It is not as popular of a web institution as some of the other sites we've discussed (Nasza-klasa, YouTube, Last.fm), but for many, especially for those interested in photography it is an important component of their online habits and part of their daily browsing routines.

According to its founders, Digart is a place to present your works, check out those of others, and, most importantly, to exchange opinions about them and expand one's knowledge about the subject. For our collaborators, it was a place to publish their photos for a larger audience, as well as their friends (and yet another chance to exchange small online friendship gestures). It is also a place to find interesting photos (to be shared with friends) and to meet new people. *That's where we met [name retracted], on Digart. She came to us there, sometimes we visit her. If there's someone from Warsaw, that's where we meet up, kind of like our friend*, Alek explains.

Digart is characterized by the fact that each account can only post a single image a day. Because of this, it is a place to publish selected photos – those considered to be the best. Not surprisingly, some of our collaborators spoke of new *Digarts* rather than of a new photos. (Digart can also be used to publish drawings or graphics but we are discussing it in terms of its use by our collaborators, who use it to share their photos and engage with a community to discuss and publish them.)

Digart comments are similar to the ones posted below pictures posted on Nasza-klasa, where attention is exchanged through brief messages that sometimes even lack text, but rather use emoticons or 'plus' signs ("+++"). In conversations with us, our young photographers expressed a distance to this type of comments, even though they themselves participated in this exchange of online gestures, and we believe that even these kinds of comments are perceived as encouragement to further pursue photography. Among these dozens of "smileys" and ritualistic exchanges of awe on our collaborators' walls, there are substantiative exchanges about lenses used, lighting or the arrangement of the compositions. Such exchanges, even if somewhat critical, can prove to be valuable. *I check more than a dozen times if somebody commented my newly added photo,* Krzysiek from Ziemielin mentioned about his emotional involvement in publicly posting his works. Alek is more aloof, but admits that sometimes it is worth taking the time to read the comments: *Sometimes some dummy writes something cool (*on my Digart profile) *or something, then, it's not a waste of time.*

Thus, photos posted on Digart perform all the functions found in other web contexts – communication, expression and performance – with the added opportunity for self-education. Even though merit-based comments do not form the majority of feedback, which is something its users know well, it is hard to question Digart's function as a source knowledge and inspiration. This is how Danek explains it: *A friend told me: 'go there and see how others take photos, you could pick up a lot that way,' and it actually is like that because you can see it from other people's perspective. That's learning from others, and sometimes committing Digart plagiarism. I had an idea for a picture but it didn't work out well, and then I can see how others did it. I'll see an idea, find a place and make a photo. It's a bit like, I'll notice that some guy made a photo like that, so I'll do my photo using his idea. It worked out pretty well.* If something's really interesting, you can ask more about it, especially if you add a bit of an ego 'stroke' to it at the same time. *You can ask questions, I usually write: 'great shot' and 'how'd you do it?' 'what lens did you use?'. Sometimes, I get questions too, I answer because I'm into it when somebody's asks me, that means it worked. Experienced users give suggestions, suggest what I could do differently. Sometimes it's not important how, critique is important, at first I'd get mad if people said 'cool, but bad focus, lacks a theme, blurry, no real vibe.'*

Our collaborators' activities, as mediated by Digart, can be understood as using new media to create communities of practice (Wenger 2006). Through Digart, our collaborators create a "group of people who share a concern or a passion for something they do and learn how to do it better as they interact regularly" (Wenger 2006). (Significantly, in communities of practice learning can, but does not have to be the primary purpose of interaction with other members). **Digart provides its community of users an architecture of communication, which lets them provide feedback, receive feedback and see the reviews received by others. The practice of sharing photos and commenting on them make up the process of group learning in a networked environment.** Maga: *I learned a lot through Digart, from reviews, from these dumb comments. For example, I kept seeing "B&W" and finally realized that's "black and white." [On Digart] you can see it all thanks to those bar graphs, if somebody has 90% in each bar graph you know that's a good photo, you look at what's in it, you can learn thanks to these evaluations.* Maga follows about 40 friends and strangers on Digart, whose photos she particularly likes.

In pre-Web times, people such as Maga or Danek could easily be termed autodidacts. *(I went to many shoots [...] I'd hear a lot about framing a shot, what a diaphragm is, thanks to these conversation, I learned what makes a good photo –* explains Maga, who never attended any photography classes). However, Maga and

Danek's presence on Digart calls into question the "auto-" part of "autodidact." The non-institutional and a-hierarchical practices mediated by Digart seem a far cry from the traditional artistic education model, but they still provide aesthetic education as well as knowledge and skills. They also call to mind the idea of a workshop, where a group of people work together, follow each other's progress and provide mutual feedback, while taking advantage of tools and knowledge which would be hard to find outside the workshop. Learning in communities of practice, as Etienne Wenger stresses, is substantially different from learning in an institutional setting: it is hard to separate the individual from the network of cooperation, it is hard to delineate learning's start and finish. It is also not like teaching – nobody is teaching anything to anybody, despite the fact that everyone is learning at the same time. Finally, it is hard to divorce this type of learning from other activities: being on Digart is part learning, part exhibition of your works, part enjoyment and part social practice which unites the online and offline spheres into one that is experienced as a single, authentic venue for your geek out.

Greniu. Listening and making music

Greniu lives in Zahaczewo. He just graduated from high school. He fondly recalls his last year in school, which, he says were like the last ball onboard the "Titanic." *When we were finally seniors, we got the feeling that we could get away with more.* To better illustrate what he's talking about, he pulls up a class movie on YouTube. It is a collage of photos and videos of school and party scenes, to the tune of *Blur*'s dynamic rock song "Song 2": people riding bicycles in school corridors, chalk fights in class, mad dancing at house parties, setting the record for the number of people in a bed during a class trip, a complicated seven-person pyramid that resembles a Chinese dragon ridden by three riders) and many others. *And that's how it looked. This captures our class's vibe and our adventures, there were more movies like this but only this one was published.*

Control-z

Music is Grenio's passion. It's his primary way of spending time, and eventually, he hopes, the way he makes his living. *I was into tons of stuff, but only making music turned out not to be a fleeting hobby. My room is an amateur recording studio, the walls are covered with sound proofing materials (carpets, Styrofoam) which I put up myself.* Grenio composes music and plays guitar in a popular local hardcore band in Zahaczewo. He's also starting a music portal with friends and getting his music production business going. He also holds informal guitar lessons. *It's mostly my friends, from scouting, from school, friends of friends know about me, so they'll sometimes ask me on GG. They come in groups or individually, and we learn various slides and chords. Most of the people are a little younger than me, but there are some older ones. Sometimes they pay, but that's pennies. Theoretically I'm giving them my time, but on the other hand, my knowledge isn't good enough to really charge a normal rate.*

Grenio's story shows how the internet can develop and deepen passions, and how it allows the development of further competencies. Grenio made his bands' website, soundproofed his room, builds guitar overdrives (distortion effects). His main guide is his cousin. *My cousin Tomek is involved in what I'd like to eventually do professionally. He's studying sound engineering and works as an acoustician. I really benefit from seeing him or talking on GG [with him]. His opinions are important to me, I really care about his point of view – a single conversation can save me dozens of hours of searching forums for answers to my questions.*

New media help him make up any knowledge shortcomings, but having someone who acts like a "master" is still invaluable. However, he can not flood his cousin with endless questions, so he frequently uses online forums and instructional movies on YouTube to figure things out. (Worth noting is the distaste for learning from text books or instruction manuals which, for many of our collaborators, is viewed as the last option.) *Looking at forums and asking questions on Elektroda.pl and DIY departments– that's my whole experience with electronics. I really wanted to have all of these guitar effects but the prices ... a single one costs like 500 złoty. So my cousin suggested: Read up on it and build one yourself. You need a bit of theory at the start, but all of that is online – both tips and theory. You've got a way of rendering a board, the arrangement of the elements, you buy the board and you build. And when you're doing it, you slowly begin to understand why this is connected here and not there, why the battery outlet is there, why this transistor – not a different one. I just brought down an old tube television from the attic, I want to use the resistors from it, which will definitely warm up a lot better than something I'd buy in a store today.* Grenio is rapidly and broadly developing his musical passion. As a small town resident with limited funds, the internet is a valuable window on the world. The web gives Grenio easy access to information, supplies (cheap components on Allegro) and contacts (free GG conversations with his cousin).

Grenio wants to study sound engineering in Cracow, but he's already taking care of producing music for young bands from the area. *Right now, that's a lot of fun for me. I love it when some punk band shows up, and then I can pick at the sound: a little louder here, slightly more bass here, a little more on the left speaker now and ... oh, yeah! But I'm still learning, I'm not a professional yet.* He prefers the trial and error type of learning. It's especially effective in a digital world where "ctrl+z" (undo) is almost always an option, and an open invitations for experiments.

Benefits of anonymity

Thanks to pursuing his hobby, Grenio has become a well known figure locally – which has its advantages and disadvantages. Grenio – along with his band – is sometimes complimented and sometimes roundly criticized. Sometimes on his band's online forum. *Unfortunately, very few people are able to provide constructive criticism. In our "guest book" there are a lot of comments like: "you guys suck!" "what are you doing here?!" or "get the fuck outta here!"* The ongoing public debate about anonymous online criticism has its local version. Grenio is used to functioning in a two-way communication climate, and presents a more nuanced view of the phenomenon. Despite venomous anonymous criticism he appreciates the benefits provided by this state of affairs and can draw meaningful commentary and feedback from it. *There are examples when somebody really tried and wrote what they liked and what they disliked about our concert. It's great to know that somebody came to see us and really listened, instead of getting hammered in front of the stage and hearing every fifth note.*

Oh! This is the best critique of our concert, Grenio points to a forum entry. *You can see that the guy really let go at the keyboard, but he accurately described the performance, a comment for the singer, the guitarist and drummer – something specific for everyone. That's probably why he wrote it here and didn't tell us face to face right after the concert, because he wanted it to be here, in one place, so that we could go back to it. And we do. And that's better than if he told us right after the gig, when I was after my third beer and whatever he said would go in one ear and fly out the other.* Grenio mentions another advantage of anonymity: on the other hand, opinions given right after a show, eye to eye, are not always honest. This varied experience with anonymous comments has affected Grenio's attitude, and allows him to draw benefits from the forum and ignoring the malcontents. *Here's a comment: 'get off the stage!' – when we were younger, something like this would really hurt us, we'd think, 'fuck, maybe the dude is right,' but with time and we've realized that we can't worry about the people who just unload their frustrations.*

I just don't download music and that's it!

Another aspect of our conversation with Grenio is related to listening, not creating, music – an important concern for a young musician. Grenio is torn on this topic. On one hand, there's a world of music available online, on the other, he would like to eventually earn money by making music and a while ago took the bold stance not to listen to pirated material. *I also want to be a musician, I want to make money from it, so if I want to make money on it and I'm stealing from others, it wouldn't be fair*, he explained. As an artist, he appreciates the promotional value of a less stringent distribution of music – his recordings are available online and are handed out at the band's concerts. He respects the will of those artists who only sell their art. As a result, Grenio is one of the few young people we met, who persistently tries not to break intellectual property laws by not downloading mp3 files online. He cleared his computer of illegal music and pirated software, switched to the Reaper shareware music production program (shareware is a type of license which describes the terms on which a program can be used for free). *I don't feel the need to use a different program, this one has everything that I need to be happy, maybe in 15 years, when I'll be a professional, I'll come to the conclusion that this one has too few features, for now, it is closer to being too much for me.*

By consciously abandoning his peers' default model of music acquisition he faces the question of getting music. In an honest life, being respectful of copyright laws is not simple. *I started by 'borrowing' some of my dad's records. Then I started buying tapes and records online on Allegro. I bought a TSA* (transl. note: 1980's Polish metal band) *record for 5 złoty. For some people it's just dad's or grandpa's garbage lying around in the attic, and they're looking to sell these 100 cassettes for 5 złoty apiece, so they make some money. For me, that's a great opportunity, because I can buy a really great album for just 5 złoty!* He also downloads many tracks which are available for free but that does not mean he isn't sacrificing a lot and that his attitude doesn't require a great deal of self-control with so many pirated temptations around. *A buddy of mine came over and plugged in his pendrive to my computer because he says I don't have any music on my hard drive. When he went to the bathroom, I was very tempted to copy an awesome album from him – a band called Heaven Shall Burn. I was thinking to myself: 'I'll copy this one album, nobody will know.' In the end, I explained to myself: 'I just don't download music and that's it!'*

For many young people listening to songs on YouTube is a way of testing a track out before downloading an mp3 file of it. Grenio, to stay true to his convictions but also to get to listen to songs he wants to hear, limits himself to listening on the video portal. *I listen to a lot of* stuff that way, but only the songs that had videos made for them. I avoid the songs that didn't have a video made for them [available on YouTube with slideshows]. Recently, Guns'n'Roses have been my favorite band and unfortunately I don't have any tape or CD of theirs. All I get by with, are their music videos on YouTube, which, obviously are free, but I'd like to listen to others songs that didn't have videos made to them.

Our conversation with Grenio shows how the intellectual property protection systems complicate the lives of people who function in a digital media world. Compared to the other young people we've introduced, Grenio, with his cautious approach to using digital media content, was a unique figure. Still, despite his impressive self-control, cautious use of digital resources and the value he attached to consuming legal content, he was also guilty of violating intellectual property rights. Reaper, the program he uses to edit music, is available for free for only one month. Also, not all of the music videos posted to YouTube are there legally. Considering the purely functional approach, we should be aware that in these digital times – even when one refuses to download illegal music – one can often violate the law or support others' illegal activities, often without even knowing it.

History – networked

Janek from Zahaczewo has been interested in local history from the 19th century onwards. He's especially captivated by the physical landmarks in the city in which he was born seventeen years ago: buildings, old advertisements, industrial objects. His passion is recreating the history of the modern world that surrounds him: *I find an old photos and try to figure out where it was taken, what was there – that's what I'm really into.*

Even though he does not live in Wrocław, he has long followed Wrocław.[domain name].com.pl, where people compile a multi-media historical compendium: posting archival or documentary photographs, audio and video recordings about surrounding towns. A year ago, a similar but smaller website was established for another local city. This prompted Janek and his younger friend Paweł to create something on their own. *We wanted to open it up to people, to gather all of these materials in one place.* The got technical advice from people from the neighboring city of Tępno. Janek bought a dedicated domain name, but used a prepared template developed by Socjum.pl. It is a service that lets people create their own social networking sites: you can selected whether it will be an open or private community, configure the desired functions (forums, galleries, user profiles, surveys, blogs), and pick the website's appearance. Thanks to it, you can quickly establish your own portal without the need to personally program web scripts: Janek and Paweł's site is DziejeMojegoMiasta.pl [domain name changed] (transl. note: My City's History.pl).

The story of the portal's development is one of the establishment and growth of relations between people of various ages, scattered around the world, whose one common bond is the city and its history. *There was no group, just the two of us.* Now, registered users include everybody from young people to retirees, among them a 70-something Zahaczewo man, a former scout, who now lives in Germany. *My dad has been involved in scouting for a long time, and at some point the local scouting group received a collection of photos from this man's scouting days in Zahaczew. Many of the photos were of the city itself. I wanted to post these photos online, but I didn't know if the man would let me. I found him on Nasza-klasa and asked, and he agreed. After that, he posted descriptions of these photos on our portal, who was who, and where they lived.* Nasza-klasa was also used as a promotional channel, helping to find the target group of local history buffs. *I asked the guy who set up a "Zahaczewo Residents" profile to promote our site. As it turns out, he collects Zahaczewo postcards, we got talking and he lives on my street, we chatted and traded some books with each other.*

As it turns out, even in small towns, within internet mediated social networks of peers, information mostly moves along well trodden paths. New media, in the first place, intensify communication with people who were already close. The net's social geography initially reproduces existing social relations. The sensation that thanks to technology we have tons of people within an arm's reach is mostly correct – but we still have to reach out to get in touch with them. In the real world, it is possible to recognize someone, exchange friendly greetings in one's apartment building or neighborhood store for years, without ever really meeting them. In the example we're describing, the two boys knew each other by sight, they were only one degree of separation removed from each other, lived close-by and yet were unaware of their shared interests. Their face to face meeting would not have occurred without the networked world (establishment of the portal, creation of the 'Zahaczewo Residents' profile on Nasza-klasa).

The project began to attract people. They added more and more materials which documented the city's everyday life. A water-works employees scanned maps from the early 20th century which he found at work. A Wrocław student from Zahaczewo, posted movies (for example, a four minute movie of an accelerated 24 hour time-lapse of the city's iconic water tower). Additional people brought in new content and ideas. Another enthusiast used Photoshop to superimpose an aerial photo onto the oldest known map of the city from 1785. *That plan is extremely accurate, you can see who owned which lots. The original is somewhere in an archive in [a neighboring city], supposedly in pretty bad shape. Thankfully, some 30 years ago, a Zahaczewo artist hand-copied the original and we used his version,* explains Janek. It is, therefore, the second 'transfer' of the original plan – all done to preserve it and share it with others. In retrospect, the copying done three decades ago was very helpful and useful.

DziejeMojegoMiasta is mostly about gathering materials that are scattered in private and institutional archives, converting them into a digital format and organizing them in a publicly accessible internet archive. In this story, the internet served as a way to organize, exhibit and gather new materials. The portal can even be credited with one historical discovery. *A while ago I stumbled onto Biblioteka Cyfrowa [digital library], it has a lot of niche books that are not available anywhere else. There, they are grouped thematically, and by keywords. If you type in 'Zahaczew,' it will find all the books that contain that name. Thanks to it, I found a German-language book on the history of the Jews in [name of region], divided up by the Jewish parishes in the region. There were two pages about the Jews of Zahaczewo.* Janek doesn't know German, but he already knew the former scout in Germany, and sent him an email with the pages. He quickly translated it, and discovered the former location of the town's mikveh – the Jewish bathhouse. *They didn't even know about it at the Zahaczewo museum.*

A town's visual archive

For Janek and other history enthusiasts of various ages and locations, new technologies – from scanners, email, Nasza-klasa, to the service which creates social networking sites – are contributing to the creation of an ever-growing interactive visual archive of the town's history. The portal currently has 251 registered users, amateur historians interested in the town's past. Janek complains that not too much is going on there. Most people just register and do not do much else. Still, the multimedia archive storing the town's past exists and continues to grow. Earlier in this report we wrote about how the perception of physical space in togetherness contexts changes when the mobile media mediated world of flowing data, emotions and images gets superimposed onto it. **Here we can see the potential of new media to help create a unique historicity of a space where our collaborators live. In this example, new media not only intensify the experience of closeness but also provide users with access to boundless sources of cultural content (in accordance with the 'connected and online' formula), and actualize events, images and emotions of the past.** Sometimes, the web does the historians' work: 'I have no clue who's in this photo,' we read below a photograph of an event that looks like a city council meeting, 'but if You would post it online, perhaps somebody will recognize someone.'

A history seen on the Web

The richness of the materials gathered on the portal is mindblowing. Your author spent more than two hours exploring the website.

1928: photo. Nineteen men with bicycles posing in front of a butcher's shop. The "Kołownicy" gathered to celebrate the 10th anniversary of Poland regaining independence. (Photo added by ..., Gadu-Gadu # ... Below the photo this comment: *People, ask your families for photos. I love looking at this types of things.*

Date not available, article scanned from a newspaper: at the last moment we learn that world-famous singer Jan Kiepura will come from [...] to [...] to sing at a folk festival; Kiepura will arrive in the afternoon in his own car

1938: a scan of a first-year report card from a local high school (religion: very good, behavior: very good, Polish language: good, physical exercises: good)

1939: a photo from the first month of WWII: a column of German trucks

Others: a boxing match in a POW camp (*I think that's where the playing field is now*, someone comments below, a scan of someone's *Ausweis* (transl. note: a German identity document) (comment below refers to references to the ID holder in books on local history

1983: a photo of a local band which performed at the Jarocin festival, both sides scanned (band members listed on the back)

1986: Photos from the opening of the 'Rolnik' (Farmer) store." *Like at a Media-Markt today*, somebody jokes below.

The student from Wrocław, whom Janek met earlier through the portal, found an invitation for bids to demolish an old slaughterhouse on the city hall's website. A small office building is planned for the site. According to enthusiasts gathered around the website, the slaughterhouse, while in bad shape, is an interesting and valuable post-industrial building. At first they considered holding a rally in front of the county administration building, but since acting quickly was most important, they decided to wage an emailing fight. They drafted a common open letter to the county executive, protesting against the demolition plans and suggesting ways of utilizing the old building. Each one of the co-authors sent it as an email to the county executive, and forwarded it to their friends, and everybody registered on the DziejeMojegoMiasta portal, asking for support. The response was quick and strong. Enough letters were sent that the official's inbox got overfilled. The next day, city hall announced that the demolition would be delayed, and asked that no more emails get sent in the matter.

Majka: a hypothesis about learning shortcuts

Majka hosts a radio show. Before each broadcast she looks over her music and compiles notes on each artist she'll feature. Hosting a show is fun, but also a lot of work. There are so many bands and songs that it's sometimes hard to find the right ones. Her playlist is varied: new stuff, recently discovered tracks, and older songs which she likes. She also takes request from listeners. Maintaining contact with her audience is important, they comment on the music being played, send wishes and debate with each other. Rastastacja (transl. note: Rasta-station) is an internet radio dedicated to reggae music. Majka just turned 18,

Music is a very important part of Majka's life. She used to listen to rock and hip-hop, but for the last year and a half she mostly listens to reggae. When she's walking around town, riding the tram by herself or handing out flyers in an underground passage, her 1 gigabyte mp3 player pulses with music. Grubson, Kacezet, PabloPavo, Ziggy Marley, Alborosie, the new Maleo Reggae Rockers... Her player mostly features Polish artists, but sometimes her headphones ring with melodic Jamaican patois.

There's a lot of new music, and it's not hard to get it. Usually a friend recommends something, sends a YouTube link through GG or an mp3 file, sometimes sends just a song title and artist – that's enough to find a track. A couple times a week, Majka goes to reggae discussion forums online. She usually doesn't contribute, but reads the discussions about records and artists. She downloads anything that seems interesting. She subscribes to *Free Colors*, the only Polish magazine dedicated to reggae. She reads interviews and record reviews, quickly using YouTube and Google to go from reading to listening to new artists.

Reggae is more than just music, it entails a certain vibe and associated passions such as making dreadlocks. Majka got into the hairstyle when, on a Roots Rock Reggae forum she found a girl from her town who knew how to twist dreads. She gave Majka her first dreadlocks. Once in a while, dreadlocks need to be maintained with a crochet hook – a difficult process. Majka found numerous descriptions on how to do it online, and started practicing on her friends' hair. She's made dreadlocks for many people, including Karol, the boyfriend of one of her friends. Another one of her passions is playing the djembe – a type of drum. Sometimes somebody brings their drum to the park or the island and Majka gets to practice a little bit, but that's not the same as having her own instrument. Majka never searched online for information about the djembe – somehow it never occurred to her – but she wanted to get one for herself. She'd like to get a large one, but big instruments are expensive, and she could learn on a small (40 cm) one, which still costs between 100 and 200 złoty. That's why she's working this summer, handing out flyers in an underground passage.

A while ago, Majka googled "radio reggae" and found the Rastastacja website. Hosts from around Poland would play music, comment on it and talk with listeners. The site also had an ad: "Rastastacja is looking for radio hosts!" She was worried that you had to be 18 to host a show. She chatted up one of the presenters on GG and it turned out that there was no age limit. Her application email had to include personal information, something about herself, why she wants to host a show, and a minute-long sample of her radio show. Majka bought a microphone, recorded a sample, it was approved and she became a presenter.

When a show is about to start, she sits down to her computer (her dad, an IT specialist, put it together), pulls out the microphone and in a sweeping motion places it on her desk. In her Opera browser, she opens the Rastastacja website and logs in as a presenter. She goes straight to the listeners' comments section and waits for the trial version of Virtual DJ, Gadu-Gadu and Rastastacja chat to open. *In the control panel there is a microphone on/off switch, and here I can see how many listeners there are...* On her desk, below a big, old CRT monitor she opens her notebook. In it, in her slightly childish handwriting, she has notes on bands, songs, and ideas for comments. Before a recent move, *I had a ten mega internet* [connection]*, and everything used to open smoothly, now things freeze up a bit and it takes some time to get everything running.* Her notepad functions as yet another window in Windows. Having it written down on paper is easier for her, *otherwise I could get a little lost.* The show starts. *I say what genre they're from, what they play, then I play a song, so that people get to know the tracks.* Deciding what to play is the most time-consuming part of the job. There are so many bands, and so many options what to play. *Each presenter has their own subject, adds a playlist, others are supposed to write what they think of the show. I like shows where I don't play anything for a while, and then I play everything I liked during that time. I know what to play and so on. Sign up for Rastastacja. You could be a presenter.*

After visiting Majka, our ethnographer, who himself plays reggae at parties in Warsaw, noted in her field notes: **I envy Majka.** *Not her knowledge of music, but how quickly she's gained her knowledge. I can see that her opportunity to access the wealth of music is incomparably easier than mine was at her age.*

What are the differences between listening to a tape copied from a friend and clicking on a YouTube link sent by a friend on Gadu-Gadu? Let's attempt to condense our ethnographic description of getting into a given hobby into a hypothesis on the new forms of cultural content circulation.

The shortcut learning hypothesis

Using the internet gives a chance to take shortcuts in learning. This means that gaining skills or knowledge becomes accelerated and more effective. One of the proofs of this acceleration is not making as many mistakes as you would without the use of the internet. You learn by others' mistakes from the past.

Taking shortcuts in learning is the product of the socio-technical aspects of internet use. As an example, we'll show several practices which definitely exist within the internet horizons of most of our collaborators. First, is the **searching for, and acquiring tutorial-type content** (both independently through Google or YouTube, or as part of the multiplication effect of the co-internet. Second **is finding and meeting people** with similar interests. Third, is **following others' conversations** (lurking – the ability to listen-in to 'expert' discussions on internet forums). Finally, there is **receiving feedback** about your efforts through grades or comments (the ability to comment is an affordance of many internet designs, in many cases, such as with Digart – it is a very prominent one).

In this way, knowledge circulating on the web continues to grow, and access to it becomes easier. This structure of cultural circulation removes many barriers associated with non-networked social groups. Perhaps Majka would not have the opportunity to learn how to make dreadlocks because she wouldn't have the opportunity to meet older people. Taking shortcuts in learning is an informal method of gathering knowledge and applying it in highly engaging areas, such as young people's passions. The mechanism appears to be a symptom of larger changes in the cultural environment.

Cultural omnivorousness?

An important feature of pop-culture is that it is split. A majority of its content, such as new generation television shows like *nip/tuck* or *house*, contain encrypted messages and references that are identifiable only by those 'in the know.' **Agata Nowotny** discusses the relationship between the cultural project known as individualization and omnivorousness with **Małgorzata Jacyno** of the Institute of Sociology at the University of Warsaw

Agata Nowotny: In its most radical version, the idea of individualization as a cultural project means that we are condemned to culture, that culture is a field of making a difference. At the same time, our research shows that the cultural choices of young Poles are incredibly difficult to predict. Traditional measures which are based on correlations between geographical location or social background and choices in music or frequency of attending the opera no longer adequately describe a society in which the status game has become much more subtle. The young people we met appear to be culturally omnivorous, absorbing very diverse cultural content.

Kamila from a small town outside of Ziemielin listens to metal, she used to even dress more 'metal.' She's also fascinated by theatre: she writes plays which she sends to nationwide contests, she tried to organize a theatre group in her town, she's seriously considering applying to a dramatic arts academy.

Taking a look at Gośka's room, we notice surprising contrasts: a *King Arthur* movie poster above her bed, and a photo of *Termin Przydatności do Spożycia* (her boyfriend's band) on her laptop's desktop. The guys in the band are inspired by "heavy" sounds: punk and hard rock. Sharing space on her bookshelf is a geography textbook, Naomi Klein's *No logo*, Carlos Ruiz Zafon's popular novel *The Shadow of the Wind*, and a classic collection of Leopold Staff (Polish poet, 1878-1957) poems published by Czytelnik. Gośka says that she'll read anything – if it interest her – she's even read a geography textbook as nighttime reading.

Narrow labels attached to subcultures do not limit the young in their musical tastes, setting the place for surprising juxtapositions. Żuku, a Metallica fan, also has a collection of jazz, reggae and blues on his computer. As one of our researchers noted after returning from the field, the young consume absolutely everything, regardless of genre and quality: from manga to *Na Wspólnej* (transl. note: a Polish soap opera).

Richard A. Peterson and Roger M. Kern used the phrase 'omnivorousness' to describe broadening tastes, which allow the assimilation of all cultural content, whether high-art or popular. What then is the difference between the cultural consumption of a high school student from Zahaczewo who's planning to study philosophy and reads scientific texts on the subject, but also frequents Demotywatory.pl, from a professor's confession that he enjoys romantic comedies?

Is omnivorousness the effect of the blurring of differences, or does it simply change its mechanisms into an even more subtle game of class status? Is cultural omnivorousness simply a game for the elites, or is it expanding into broader social spectrums?

Małgorzata Jacyno: I find it hard to accept the theory of "omnivorousness," or at least its simplest understanding suggesting a collapse in distinctions and symbolic distances. I wouldn't want to repeat the popular discussions of new methods of constructing pop-culture content, in which, there are at least two narratives, one of which is understandable only to those "in-the-know" – those with appropriate cultural capital. In other words, pop culture is "splitting." The great majority of this new cultural content (for example, new generation television shows such as *Nip/Tuck*, and to a lesser extent *House*) contains built-in, encrypted content and quotes which are understood by the "chosen ones."

"Omnivorousness" was described by Pierre Bourdieu as a specific strategy of some members of the French "middle class" (of course, the French sociologist did not use this expression). It appears that Bourdieu's arguments dealing with cultural diversity as a place where class distances appear can be related to what we are currently seeing, and "omnivorousness" can be perceived as both a specific strategy as well as another stage in symbolic wars. I want to remind that "middle class" is a sense of coherence and that it encompasses very diverse positions and aspirations. Here, among this "middle class" is where the battles over "distinctions" are most bitter and ferocious. Besides, we are most likely talking about different versions of "omnivorousness." The small town teenager who watches *Klan* (transl. note: a Polish soap opera) and reads philosophy books is similar to that big city professor. For the girl, her cultural "trips" are the philosophical treatises, while, for the professor, a TV show can be the same kind of a "trip." "Omnivorousness," or rather the appearance of omnivorousness is based on the intensity of conflicts, and experimental tendencies of the "middle class," as well as from a change in the location of cultural "secrets."

Following the spirit of Bourdieu's sociology, we can say that just as there are social strata which posses enough economic capital to act prodigally and indulge in mind-bending profligacy, there are groups who posses enough cultural capital to spend it freely. Some buy unconscionably expensive watches and 'waste money' that way, others are able to do the same with a different resource: cultural capital. Therefore, there are people whose cultural capital is so big, that they can act completely "un-economically" ("crazily"), as if their lives were so full of these precious commodities. These seemingly "un-economic" methods of symbolic combat, can be extremely effective in the symbolic sense. We can even consider the existence of a new type of style among some of the "middle class" fractions, which is connected to this "conspicuous spending" of cultural capital. The fascination with Bollywood and Turkish cinema's "Star Wars" variations are some of the notable examples of this conspicuous consumption. It is worth noting that during these "worst movies in the world" festivals (such series have recently begun to appear at various film festivals) one can listen to lectures by distinguished and avant-garde film critics.

Lower class culture is becoming extremely attractive. A part of the "middle class," the one that never worried it would be mistaken for the lower classes, build its whole identity on, as Bourdieu called it, a cult of pop. The emancipatory spirit of the "middle class" allowed them to free themselves of the doubly limiting sense of morality. Fleeing "middle class aesthetic" is a moment of actualization of a life strategy adopted by that part of the middle class whose life goal is escaping social classifications. Thus, on one hand we can talk of a significant change: the middle class wants to free itself of the aesthetic sensibility that is ascribed to it. On the other hand, as Bourdieu noted, the celebration and manifestation of individual, personal, and unique manias, fixations and oddities is a characteristic of this social class. People say that class distances have fallen away. It used to be that researchers struggled to pinpoint social practices which people felt ashamed of, especially if they were part of those viewed as particularly "regressive" – such as watching television. Today, the "middle class" ostentatiously admits to its "faults," or choices deemed "undistinguished" and "unrefined." We must remember to keep reflexivity in mind here. Psychology, sociology, and philosophy have become commonplace. Middle class "moral inhibitions" became thematized as just that in numerous fashions and in numerous discourses. The initial moral, and currently aesthetic, freedom is a continuation of identity searches and problems. A viewer can watch a romantic comedy because it was created "especially for him." Another, can look-in on it, because he's ashamed of his feelings which were stirred by what is broadly termed "shallow" content, and is afraid of both publicly risking his cultural capital and his own self-image. Then, we have a third viewer who is moved by the romantic comedy and ignores any possible accusations of a lack of emotional depth and inclusion among the "damned." He knows that the church he belongs to, is invisible, and the saved differ from the damned – to utilize Weber's arguments to explain cultural practices – only by their consistent, inner faith that they will be saved.

Still, "omnivorousness," as presented in the above examples, is not evidence of a blurring of symbolic boundaries or a "peace treaty" among classes and fractions of the "middle class," as much as it is evidence that below the atmosphere of play, irony and pastiche hide equally brutal battles over re-creating distances and marking new class divisions. Some cross these boundaries while knowing next to nothing about them due to their lack of cultural knowledge. Others, have made an art out of walking these narrow dividing lines. One is reminded of Goffman's phrase that even adults like to take a spin on the merry-go-round once in a while.

But, they do so in different ways: some are discomforted by engaging in this child-like amusement, some enjoy the ride while overtly manifesting their detachment from the 'unworthy' amusement, while the third group can enjoy the forbidden fruit of childish joy without worry. Only these last ones are truly enjoying themselves, because only they know that the first group's self-consciousness is "best" proof that they have fears connected to some form of regression or lack of self control. In order to really "lose yourself" in a situation, one must know that one does not risk getting stuck in it, that one can get out of any state of "cultural regression" by their own powers.

I have two concluding comments.

First, I'll simply underline that youth is an increasingly culturalized category. Youth content refers to everything that was ascribed to young people in the 1950s. It is the most "anarchic" category and thus the one most appropriate for "middle class" stylizations of those of its fractions which want to avoid classification the most. I would describe "omnivorousness" as a style of controlled anarchy.

Second, pop culture has become the storage space for forbidden or marginalized content. V. Nelson, among others, wrote about this. Wonder, unbelievability (also passivity and all forms of regression – such as dependency) carry the most potential for transgressions. (Perhaps the fascination with medical dramas stems from the fact that a patient is by definition passive and dependent.) In other words, emancipation (or perhaps just criticism) involves a symbolic return to all things that represent the archaic and folk – to "primitive culture" when it was nearly indistinguishable from the state of nature. Omnivorousness can then be interpreted as a refusal to classify choices or to engage in classifiable (by social scientist) choices.

Małgorzata Jacyno

AT SCHOOL

The appearance of new media in school environments does not only change old practices (like hallway conversations, group study, exchange of class notes and cheating). It also raises new problems, one of the biggest being the credibility and truthfulness of internet-sourced knowledge in a school context. The communication architecture of new media helps group efforts in solving (or avoiding) problems, sharing resources and competencies. It also presents a significant challenge to an educational system which evaluates and promotes individual achievements. In this chapter we ask how school rules and hierarchies change when teachers and students begin acting in a networked world.

We followed our collaborators to school. They were returning from two months of vacation, some of us returned after more than 10 years. Our return to school did not shock us with obvious changes: the characteristic layout of classrooms and hallways stayed the same, we saw the same ferns in the flower pots, the green chalkboards of our youth were still streaked with permanent chalk marks, the familiar photos of great national authors hung on the walls, and VHS tapes with Sienkiewicz's *The Flood* still sat in glass cases. The unavoidable sense of nostalgia made an impression, despite the fact that the lives of many of the young people going to school are much different from our's a decade ago. Physically the schools remained relatively unchanged. But, as we explored new school realities, we realized that changes are happening below the surface, invisible at first glance.

Generally speaking, a school's main function is organizing access to knowledge and creating an environment which encourages its absorption. Teachers are still responsible for implementing a centralized plan of instruction. School is a space, at the center of which lays the hierarchical teacher – student relationship. This relation is the fundamental avenue for transferring sanctified knowledge in the school system. This hierarchical relationship is built on a double asymmetry: first, the legitimization of knowledge (a school knows what's worth knowing, and students do not have a say in it), second, on access to knowledge (the teacher knows, a student learns). As our studies show, both asymmetries which are an important element of functional model of a school are facing changes.

Media under the desk

From the students' perspective, school is not only a place to gain knowledge but also, simply, a place where they spend a lot of time. Practices related to the didactic process are intertwined with socializing, negotiating hierarchies, and the formalization and standardization of the learning process. This is why, for our collaborators and their friends, school is also a space where various types of intertwined relationships exist: teachers, students, classes, groups of friends. It is a web of relationships within an institution, but also often extending beyond it. It is a web in which likes and dislikes mix, authority figures mix with laughable ones. School has its own time and emotional rhythms, which are a point of reference for the rest of the day, and are marked by getting there, lessons, breaks and "after school" time. Schools are also significant spots on a city's map, sharing neighborhoods with a space marked by familiar walls, classrooms, cabinets and traditional break and after class meeting points.

New media play a significant and ambiguous role in each one of these dimensions. Used more, or less, skillfully, creatively or efficiently, they create new opportunities and present new problems. In our discussions about the role of new media in schools we wanted to leave aside the obvious question of multi-media use as part of the learning process. We are doing so because it is a broad and complex topic, and a proper analysis of it would require a deeper understanding of the educational system and learning theories than we posses. Yet, we are convinced that the significance of new communication technologies in the cultural transformation of school environments cannot be limited to the narrow category of "multimedia." We also do not focus on computer science classes as a separate "problem," because it is an educational subject that is relatively far removed from the everyday practices related to using the ever-present new media. This chapter is dedicated to analyzing the presence of media at various levels of school relationships and to highlighting the ways in which bottom-up phenomena involving them are affecting the existing educational model. Therefore, we are interested in how new media are used in every aspect of school life except classroom instruction. We believe that our observations and the resultant knowledge could be useful in thinking about school and teaching at an institutional level.

Rapidshare *Iliad*

The digital world is infiltrating the school world. At the institutional level, the process of mediating schools is manifested by computer science courses or computer labs. At the level of individuals who participate within schools (students and teachers), we encountered officially sanctioned new media practices (reports written on a computer, PowerPoint presentations, the use of multimedia projectors during class). Following our collaborators, we found a broad sphere of varied group or individual practices, carried with or without teachers' approval or even knowledge. The phrase "got on the internet," in the educational context at least, has almost uniformly negative connotations. However, as it turns out, students do not look to the internet as just a source of questionable ready solutions.

Żuku would much rather listen than read. *When we had to read The Iliad at school, I couldn't manage it. It was very rough going. So I would fire up an audiobook and read along with the speaker and it went a lot better. They read at a pace you can keep up with reading for yourself.* He downloaded the audiobook from Rapidshare, a service he usually uses to get his favorite bands' music. Rapidshare is a service which allows users to make their files available to others for downloading. Żuku could have been downloading Metallica mp3s at the same time as Homer's masterpiece. When reading, Żuku sits at his desk, one hand on the mouse controlling the playback, the other, turning the book's pages.

internet applications also simplify group work and mutual help. Before a physics test, Marianna starts studying by herself. Then she meets up with a friend on Skype, solving problems together, asking questions, repeating formulas, and fine-tuning their knowledge. This way, Marianna saves time by not going to her friend's house, saves money by not calling her on the phone, while still benefiting from studying together. All, while she still checks out new comments on her friends' photoblogs.

High schoolers do not need Nasza-klasa to find long-lost classmates, but the website has also become useful in organizing school-related activities. Reading lists, absence information, and class schedules are all posted on each class's Nasza-klasa forum. While checking out friends' new photos and comments, a student can see if a teacher posted the homework assignment on the class forum. On Kamila's class forum, there's a thread titled "Class calendar" which lists scheduled tests and exams. *Pola used to carry a calendar with her, she would write down everything, while we would do so in our notebooks. We would always ask her what was coming up, and she'd post it on Nasza-klasa. Finally, she started posting it all there and others would add other things. Even teachers use it, and post due-dates.* Maintaining the class forum has become one of the responsibilities of class officers (usually the class representative or treasurer handles it). The photography skills honed while taking photos for Nasza-klasa, are making the school photographer redundant. It is usually one of the students who handles the responsibilities.

Rule of the algorithm

The most common way of using the internet we witnessed were individual searches for information necessary to prepare for lessons. Gośka, even though she has tons of books at home, simply searches the internet when preparing to give a presentation in class – it's easier and more manageable that way. However, she does not fully trust online information sources. This is why, after typing in her search into Google, she opens several tabs in her browser to evaluate the search results. She only uses information that appears on multiple websites, as repetition lends the results more credibility. *I paste some stuff in, write other stuff in my own words, I use intelligent pasting*, she explains. She takes her teachers' warnings about unreliable internet sources seriously after one particularly unpleasant experience. She once handed in a history paper based entirely on online sources and she later learned that all the dates she used were incorrect.

The trustworthiness of online information sources can be problematic for our young collaborators. It is worth noting this, and proposing the following hypothesis: the risk involved in using sources less reliable than traditional printed materials is understood by today's students and is calculated into their practices. Finding reliable information online has become an exercise in common sense, and students use various methods to minimize the risks involved. People are more willing to take risks when dealing with the 'less important' subjects that are not covered on high school graduation exams.

The criteria for evaluating reliability are diverse, and new media are introducing new methods of evaluating sources.

For a top student like Gośka, searching for information online is not the first instinct, but rather, an emergency option when her textbooks do not provide answers. *The internet is good because it is faster, but nothing on it is reliable. You never know if [the information] is based on reality. Anyone can write something, it could be a professor or somebody that has no clue. I try not to use Wikipedia, and rather use the encyclopedia at Onet.pl Wiem (transl. note: a leading Polish portal's educational branch). For the most part, it's school information, for example, with physics – for which I don't have textbooks – I check stuff out online. I do a Google search, open three pages, and after I check them I can be sure. I compile from several definitions, a bit from here, a bit from there, the top search results are the best.* Clearly, the key problem in using the internet for learning is competency of judging the value of retrieved information. While traditional publications are somewhat 'grounded' by the publisher's selection process, who – theoretically – provides a guarantee of quality (by publishing texts which were favorably reviewed or at least went through a proofreading process), online publications can be ephemeral, anonymous and lacking any editing or proofing.

Comparing content from various sources and trusting the information which is repeated most frequently is the most popular strategy for dealing with this problem. However, this approach also has its faults, especially in a digital world, where copying and compiling content of other websites is commonplace. Another method, suggested by the first approach, is ranking websites by their reliability.

Janek from Zahaczewo prefers using Wikipedia. He participated in the creation of several historical entries himself, and understands the site's process of collective editing and compiling knowledge (more about Janek on p.133-5). Anyone can become an entry's co-author, and edit the contents of an article, but, at the same time, this input is constantly being verified by others who are also interested in the subject. The clarity of the editing process allows for checking who added which content and when – by clicking on a sub-page of a Wikipedia article one can familiarize themselves with the controversies and comments on the subject. He does not trust the most popular cheat-sheet portal (Sciaga.pl [transl. note: "ściąga" means crib]) at all: *nobody knows who writes these texts, and besides, they are usually rather mediocre.* On the other hand, Wikipedia, when treated as a not-fully trustworthy encyclopedia (one checks not only a single entry, but also the process of its development), can be quite useful. Some articles are much more detailed than they would be in a traditionally published compendium. Gośka, more or less consciously, relies on the wisdom of Google's algorithms: the higher the result's placement, the more 'authoritative' it becomes. (Clay Shirky wrote about the cultural domination of algorithms in the pursuit of knowledge, 2009). Her trust is conditional, she trusts a source only if other sources (also provided by Google search results) confirm the information in it.

Besides Wikipedia, the Onet encyclopedia and Sciaga.pl, we did not come across other web-institutions which would be among the initial sources of school knowledge. For the most part, students rely on *ad hoc* Google search results, which are used when they appear on the results page.

...That's when I ask uncle Google

On a more general level, Janek and Gośka's methods of finding information are quite similar. They are both relying on various forms of distilled collective authority. With Wikipedia, it is the result of direct actions of the encyclopedia's users, who re constantly modifying and verifying the content. The search engine's mechanism relies on the automatic processing of information gathered from the actions of thousands of internet users (the basis for Google rankings is the number of sites linking to a given page in the context of a specified keyword). The collective authority mechanism which dominates online information searches ("everyone can contribute, and the majority cannot be wrong") is the inverse of the traditional method of organizing knowledge ("the experts can not be wrong") – which is reproduced in educational institutions.

Most of the students we met declare their skepticism about the online model of reproducing knowledge. *I sometimes use Wikipedia, but from what I hear it's not a good source of information, because anyone can write anything on there. Our history teacher once told us about Wikipedia mistakes in dates and events. I trust him and know he knows a lot about history*, Paweł told us. On the other hand, when he needs information: *that's when I ask uncle Google, I talk to him if I want to find out about something and don't know a site where I could directly find an answer*. In practice, everyone who searches for information online is relying on collective authority. This has its effects on the school's authority, and therefore the authority of a teacher who acts as an expert who dispenses hierarchically-approved knowledge. In our conversations with them, young people clearly stated the desire to work with teachers who possessed broad knowledge of the subjects they are teaching. That's when the students could rely on the knowledge – to a large extent. For their part, teachers admit to feeling additional pressure from knowledge that a student could check the accuracy of what they are teaching while still in class. The situation is particularly challenging for long-tenured teachers: once, there were class know-it-alls who enjoyed pointing out the teacher's mistakes or lack of knowledge, but now, with internet available on mobile phones – every student becomes a potential know-it-all. The establishing of teachers as infallible experts in their fields creates tensions on both sides of the school barricade.

Anyone can write, anyone can correct

The teachers with whom we spoke, or about whom our collaborators told us, have an extremely varied attitude toward new media. They often appreciate the opportunities offered by digital technologies, while equally frequently expressing worries about the information that can be found online, and students' practices aimed at subverting the process of testing the acquisition of knowledge.

A Polish language teacher told us about a student who answered a test question incorrectly after relying on information he found in an online source. After getting the test back, with his wrong answer appropriately marked, he brought in a printout from the website as ultimate proof that he was right. *Students sometimes treat Wikipedia as the absolute arbiter of truth, I often hear 'but that's what it said on Wikipedia,'* recalls Katarzyna, a Polish language teacher who sees the danger, not so much in using online resources, as in placing unquestioned trust in them. Agata told us about her history teacher who is dead-set against Wikipedia, and made it his mission to dissuade students from using it as a resource. *He hates Wikipedia, when a student is giving a presentation, he sits with a laptop and checks if the student is repeating sentences found online, that's when he fails you.*

We met teachers who treat all online sources as unreliable. One of our collaborators has a computer science teacher who's worked for 16 years, in a conversation with our researcher she claimed: *When students search on Wikipedia, they place complete trust in everything that's written there. My duty is to steer them away from this mistake, because things can't be like that. As I've always said: the internet is a trash can. [...] As a homeroom teacher I told the students we could take a class trip, but they would have to organize it all. They went online and found a place for 15 złoty a night, outdoor bathroom, disgusting blankets, but the 'resort's' photos were so nice that we 'just had to go.' For the next trip, I made them do a reconnaissance visit. They learned that the internet is not a reliable source of information.*

We frequently came across teachers' distaste for Wikipedia. It was the focus of attacks on the reliability of online sources – complaints about the well-developed online market for study guides and cheat-sheets have receded in significance. The primary complaint about the online encyclopedia was that it is "full of mistakes," but instead of specific examples we were mostly offered the standby phrase "anyone can write anything they want on it." Seemingly, the teachers' attitude towards Wikipedia is based on a general lack of trust for an unusual model of spreading knowledge, which, intuitively, can seem nonsensical – and thus, in the teachers' minds, must provide faulty results. Meanwhile, Wikipedia's model – in addition to the "anyone can write anything" aspect, also features an "anyone can correct" mechanism – appears to result in shockingly positive results. Studies which compared the online encyclopedia's frequency of errors compared to traditional printed ones, showed that both sources contain a comparable amount of mistakes (Giles 2005). It is also worth considering that Wikipedia articles which cover the canons of mainstream knowledge (the articles school students are most likely to be using) are closer to broad encyclopedia articles than simple encyclopedia entries. (For example, the entry for *Pan Tadeusz,* a classic Polish novel-length poem, numbers over 20,000 characters – over 10 pages of standardized text).

Wikipedia contains only encyclopedic knowledge, the type that in an idealized learning process would act as a compass – helping to translate knowledge into understanding – a critical part of the learning process. It is worth examining whether the art of careful and reasonable use of this new, but already broadest and most popular source of knowledge known to mankind, wouldn't be more useful than actively fighting it.

Educational WWW

Drawing knowledge directly from the internet is only one aspect of teachers' attitudes toward new media. Paweł, a 30 year old ethics teacher at a Ziemielin high school, completed a course in html and php programming languages and Adobe Dreamweaver (an application which creates graphics and animation for websites) during summer vacation. Paweł asked his friend *who runs an educational website* to provide him with some space on his server, and created his own page, posting information for his high school and college students. Having a personal website allows him to quickly revise content and avoid needless bureaucracy. Otherwise, he'd have been dependent on the school's IT specialist, who is also responsible for computer science classes and does not receive extra pay for running the school's website. There is a link on the high school's official page to Paweł's site. On it, Paweł posted detailed instructions for writing the end of the semester paper (for example: "Nobody willingly chooses to do wrong" claimed Socrates. Explain how you interpret this sentence"), exam topics ("Differences in Plato and Socrates' ethical conceptions"), reading lists and links to outside sources. Additionally, he posts information for students participating in philosophy and arts Olympiads (including essays by students who participated in previous years – "Explain the meaning of happiness from the perspective of modern man," written for the 20th Philosophy Olympiad). *This is the educational system's dilemma: when somebody forces you to learn something, you defend yourself, if you're interested in something, knowledge comes easily and you're not looking at your watch, you're so involved in the thing [...] students should be steered toward certain topics,* Paweł says. His website has a simple appearance, it is entirely written in html, but he's planning to add scripts to it, thanks to which it will have expanding menus, which will force users to pose specific questions by choosing the appropriate category.

Paweł tries to teach his students how to think logically and critically. That's what he looks for in their papers, as well as the ability to create proper bibliographies. He allows quotes from Wikipedia (he participated in the creation of the encyclopedia's entry for Wittgenstein), but warns them that articles using just that source can be very basic and do not cover topics in entirety. Some of the books his students need are not widely available. Paweł tries to scan portions of texts used in class. His students gave him an illegal copy of Fine Reader, a program which transforms large image files into a smaller, searchable PDF file. We should note that Paweł actively receives and sends digital and digitized media online. A student brings in a downloaded mp3 of Indian music on his mobile phone so that the whole class can listen during a lesson on Indian culture. A former students sends along a PDF of an interesting book. Paweł, in turn, burns CDs for his students with his favorite mp3s, mostly industrial, noise and ambient music.

Gośka's teacher runs an e-learning platform with history and social studies materials. Students use one email address and a shared password, thanks to this they have access to a virtual shared hard drive: whatever one of them posts there can be accessed by the whole class. Homework questions are posted on the account, to be printed out and filled in, or returned to the teacher via email, students also get texts and notes to prepare for tests. *We don't just learn from the textbook, I don't know where he [teacher] gets the articles he sends us*, said Gośka.

Building a community around specific websites or forums, can also be an impulse for shared actions. This is illustrated by the following tale from a prestigious high school in Parna. One of the teachers ran a popular, unofficial school website. It featured things such as so-called lucky numbers (students with those numbers would not get called on that day in class), in-depth information about school events, and links to students' photo galleries. The site functioned as a natural extension of school life, it was also used by parents and alumni, and became one of the most important sites in our collaborator's online lives. The students perceived a negative attitude toward it from school administrators, who viewed it as being out of their control. When the site went down during a server malfunction, gossip and anger quickly spread among students. The students were convinced that the administration was behind the shutdown and printed up stickers with the slogan "[site name] – isn't dead," and wore black shirts in protest. There was also discussion of the event in the online forum of the local edition of Gazeta.pl (most popular Polish daily newspaper), which included over 300 entries. *I explained to them that the principal didn't ban the site, but they wouldn't believe me – that's when I realized how important the site was*, one teacher recalled. Surprised by the students' protests, school officials quickly asked the website's administrator to run an officially sanctioned version of it as well (for no additional compensation). As we can see, school events which challenge the hierarchical model of schools are not solely students' doing. Even teachers occasionally act outside the official school structures.

School outside of school

The appearance of new media has resulted in the decline of traditional forms of communication, which used to announce lesson plans, parent-teacher conferences or school ceremonies.

Aldona is a 35 year old Polish language teacher. She is the class tutor for a computer science-focused class. Her students are frequent internet users. She gave them her Gadu-gadu number, they know her email address, and are among her 267 Nasza-klasa friends. During the summer after graduating middle school, her soon-to-be students joined her class's Nasza-klasa profile. Curious, she checked out their profiles on the service. She was careful not to read any forum discussions. *A colleague of mine was shocked when she saw* [on Nasza-klasa forum discussions] *very vulgar and crude comments, and then the same girls would be sitting in the front row of her class, answering every question and being extremely polite. There are things you're better off not seeing*, she adds. *I'm also a different person when I get out of class and go out on the town with my friends.* It's 9 p.m., Aldona turns on her computer to do some more work. **On her GG status she writes: Tomorrow is the final day to hand-in excused absence notes. She knows that they'll bring them in tomorrow, as her students sit online non-stop.** There's an immediate 'new message' beep on GG: *oh, good evening, you're not asleep yet Ma'am? what are you doing Ma'am?* A moment later: *What time's the parent-teacher conference, my mom's asking?* Even if her profile is *asleep* she gets messages: *maybe you're there Ma'am?* Aldona lacks the strength to answer every question, she can not get any work done when's she's constantly interrupted on GG. Eventually, she closes her GG account. Since that time, whenever she wants to communicate with her class, she calls the class president, who posts it on some forum online. Aldona's colleague, an ethics teacher, also closed his GG account, because the teenagers would constantly start chatting to him. However, he responds to students' emails as late as 3 a.m.

This situation allows us to state a broader problem. A teacher that wants to maintain contact with his pupils, is drawn into a reflexive, declarative and practical defining of boundaries and is forced to clarify the practices of using new media in his relations with his students. The school can not expect him to use an internet communicator, but in his students' eyes a teacher who is at ease with new technologies benefits both as an authority figure willing to answer questions, and as a person who belongs to the students' technology-infused world which encourages intensive contacts and consumption of multimedia cultural content.

Katarzyna, another Polish language teacher recalls: *I got my first cell phone from my students at the end of the school year. They said they wanted to send me text messages from their vacations, and the phone had their numbers already entered into it. They knew that at that point I was very much against mobile phones, but they gave it to me as a gift that I couldn't refuse. At first, they flooded me with messages, partially as a joke – I think, but then they grew out of it.* This was a few years ago, each year new grades of students come into the school, and Katarzyna always gives her email address and cellphone number on the first day of school. The initial flood of messages repeats itself every year. They treat these communication channels like all the others, for them it's like stopping me in the hallway and asking me a question. The fact that they don't understand the difference is obvious when they call after 11 p.m. or on Sunday – I now turn off my ringer at night. She quickly adds: they don't do it out of a lack of respect, they just don't sense these boundaries, but when you explain to them, once or twice, they recognize it.

Wherever new media enter the school world, student-teacher relations tend toward a more symmetrical arrangement, one encouraged by new media themselves. During first lessons with a new teacher, students often get her email address, Gadu-gadu number and sometimes cellphone number. They intensively use these means of communication everyday, they're accustomed to the idea that if they want to get to know someone better, they contact them immediately. Thus, what a student views as a simple chat on GG (like dozens of others) can represent a breaking of privacy boundaries to the teacher receiving the message. These boundaries are becoming more and more blurred, more so than even a few years ago.

As Agata was telling us about her school, she showed us her Polish language teacher's photo on Nasza-klasa. In the sun-dappled pic, a woman is sitting on a red motorcycle with a man hugging her, gently biting her on her exposed arm (*that's a cool photo, from her Honeymoon trip, they went on a motorcycle tour of the Balkans,* **explains Agata**). Doubtlessly, the teachers who educated this report's authors shared tender moments with their spouses, but back then it was much easier to keep these moments entirely out of their students' eyes. Our online existence is mostly easily accessible to others which blurs the boundaries between the private and public spheres of life. To the students, it is natural that their teachers would post these kinds of photos on Nasza-klasa. Equally natural, is the desire to chat with a teacher on GG. The students are cognizant that this works both ways, and that teachers have much easier access to their out-of-school lives. This is apparently non-problematic. *We're, you know, old enough that we don't really have any ambitions towards our teachers, so we don't really have too much to hide,* claims Alek.

The commingling of private and public spheres in a school environment forces everyone to evaluate which type of an interaction a particular action belongs to. Anyone, no matter how old or skillful in using new media, can make a mistake. At Krzysiek and Alek's school, the server had an unofficial discussion forum used only by students. This lent a misleading sense of privacy to the discussions. As Alek recalls, *Krzysiek criticized the English teacher once – that her lessons are badly organized and that she's ugly – or something like that. It wasn't constructive criticism but more emotional. A few months later, the teacher chewed him out in* front of the whole class, and he didn't even know what she was talking about. He had already forgotten the post and had to look it up later to remember.

In school environments, new media mostly function in the teacher-student relationship. However, their impact is also noticeable in the teacher-student-parent triangle. If a student is absent for several days without an excuse, is now seen as an unusual event. The teacher has access to parents' email and cellphone numbers, and can quickly verify the reasons for the absences and possibly take action. On the other hand, some teachers complained that parents who have access to an e-gradebook or a class forum, know that the teacher can contact them whenever she wants and they do not show up for parent-teacher conferences which remain an important element of school and class organization, and help build parent-teacher relations. Thus, new media allow quick access in specific and pressing matters, but, for some parents, function as an excuse from active participation in their child's education, or school and class matters.

Two clicks away from distraction

In discussing the functioning of "school outside of school" we want to briefly look at the significant question of individual study at home. Using new media to study at home creates a problem: the proximity of temptations. When discussing her experiences during the 24 hour new media abstinence experiment, Agata noted with surprise that homework without internet access took less time than usual. She discovered for herself, how much of her 'homework time' is spent doing things unrelated to school, and directly related to sitting in front of a computer.

Most of our collaborators do their homework in their rooms. Either with a computer (because the assignment is posted on a Nasza-klasa forum, because a presentation has to be made, because papers are better printed out, because my friend's notes are scanned), or at least in its proximity (the computer is usually on 'just in case' – for music, for Gadu-Gadu, to check something on Google or Wikipedia).

I tell myself that I gotta finish two essays ... but once I sit in front of the computer, I find a hundred more important things to do, Łukasz told us. Olka Gołdys who spent two weeks with the young people of Parna, described it this way: *they come back home from school, and while waiting for their parents and dinner they watch TV or do their daily roundup of 'their' websites – this is their chilling out/resting after school time. Then, after dinner, they go to their room, sit in front of the computer and the fight begins: me and school (homework, studying, books, notebooks) versus me and the internet (Demotywatory, Facebook, Nasza-klasa, YouTube, Allegro, Gadu-Gadu and its links and friends who are also sitting in front of their computers with a wavering desire to study).*

Procrastination is a psychological term describing a pathological tendency to constantly put off certain activities for later. Psychologists trace its roots to stifled fears. It appears that the common and intensive use of digital media might be making procrastination a social phenomenon. When looking up information online, young people are always two clicks away from a place that has nothing to do with studying. Along with the spread of computers we've found ourselves in a difficult spot where our primary work tool is also the primary means of entertainment. In this way, work and study time is constantly commingled with entertainment and relaxation time.

Text message test

Up to now, we have focused on students' new media practices mostly dealing with knowledge acquisition and coordination of school life. We wrote about practices, which while not always fitting with schools' desires, nonetheless worked within teachers' and schools' stated purpose. However, our collaborators frequently used new technologies to circumvent their schools' efforts to test the knowledge they acquired.

Maga always cheats in chemistry class. Despite being in a bio-chem focused class – she just doesn't get it. Along with a friend, she's developed a paper and text message cheating system for copying from one of her girlfriends who sits two desks away. First, she copies test questions onto a sheet of paper which she passes along to her friend. From the teacher's desk, the view of Maga copying the test questions looks exactly like Maga working on the problems. Sending these questions by text message, Maga would put herself at a lot of risk – her teacher knows she's not good at chemistry, and getting caught cheating with a cellphone can result in strict penalties, including having the phone taken away from her during class until the end of the year. On the other hand, her friend, one of the best chemistry students in the class, doesn't raise any cheating suspicions by typing a text message during a test. Maga's phone is on top of her desk, leaning on her pencil case, angled so that she only has to glance at the screen to read an incoming message. She doesn't even have to touch the device.

The most startling descriptions that we came across, dealt with situations where a teacher – due to his lack of competency with mobile technologies – looses control of a class, and students end up exploiting the situation. One of the high schoolers with whom we spoke to described it this way: *I got tests so figured out, that even when I don't know what I'm writing about, I still get a 5* (transl. note: On a 1-6 scale). *Somebody in class sent me a link which had the answers to the test we had the next day. One time one of my buddies had a laptop [in school], took the teacher's pendrive, and copied three years worth of tests. Here at [name withheld] high school we've had the same tests for the last three years, so we have photos of these tests and we can trade them between different classes. That's why we have time to play around.*

At the Zahaczewo high school, the computer lab has had the internet for a long time (even the oldest students do not remember when it happened). During the recent refurbishing of the school's office suite, the decision was made to install a WiFi network to avoid computer chord tangles. Students from the IT-specialization class, who helped install the network, now use the school's free internet on their cell phones (at least those with more advanced devices). Since the network was meant to be used in the offices, it does not reach all areas of the school building. For that reason, exams written in classrooms close to the principal's office are much less stressful than **tests taken far from the router**.

The theme of bypassing teachers' expectations came up frequently during our researchers' conversations with the young people. *Recently, I've been going more and more with the internet on my mobile phone, when I'm writing something for a grade at school* – claims Alek. *The teachers don't know that you can cheat through a phone*. Kuba adds the following: *if you got a paper cheat-sheet, the teacher doesn't hesitate to grab it and keep it as proof. The phone is more difficult: with one press of a button I can go back to the main menu, and no teacher would dare search through my phone, so he's not sure if I was cheating or just checking the time.*

Mobile phone communications have another advantage: they go directly to the addressee. This eliminates the in-betweens necessary in traditional "pass it on" note-passing system, which often created a lot of 'static' in the lines of communication. Marianna remembers a time when a girl in her class refused to pass on a cheat-sheet with test answers that was making its rounds in class. The girl claimed she was afraid of being caught by the teacher. Marianna suspects she just didn't want everybody else to have the right answers. A cellphone armed with cheap messages also helps spread less risky content. During a boring history class, a student can think up a brilliant "a Pole, a Russian, and a German walk into a bar" type joke and share it with all his classmates. The text message itself can become a joke, as Alek proved in one history class. All of his classmates received a text message that read: "Who drew that elephant on the ceiling?" He was laughing it up when he saw the number of heads looking up. *An SMS is better than a note, because a note can be intercepted and a text messages can't*, he confirms.

Ethnographic field reports allow us to move beyond the stereotypical dichotomy in which a "good student" uses the internet "correctly" and learns more effectively, while a "bad student" cheats during tests and plagiarizes essays. Some of the young people we met think of school as another type of service, which they desire, but it does not always fulfill their individual preferences or expectations. The questions of which teacher does his job well, which subjects are useful, which classes are interesting, were the subjects of many conversations among students graduating from high school. The way in which they act online, reflects the students' general choice of strategy. On occasion, one person can use the internet in a very basic (copy & paste) style to pass subjects which he does not care about or will not take on graduation exams, and, at the same time, be very competent and subtle in taking advantage of online opportunities to expand his knowledge in subjects he finds interesting or significant.

Student – teacher: relations mediated by media

The influence of new media on school environments mostly manifests itself in two areas. First, it affects the way in which students organize and use knowledge in the school context, and second, it shifts student-teacher relationships toward a partnership model. Both of these phenomenons seem to be largely connected to the spread of new technologies throughout society.

The teacher's position as the one who (unilaterally) presents students with content that they must master is eroding. In a situation where both students and teachers have access to immense stores of information, teachers are frequently placed in contexts where students introduce them to facts, new sources of knowledge or skills. Utilizing new media in the learning process strengthens partnerships between students and teachers. In the context of these, more partner-like, relations, teachers are more appropriately viewed as competent actors, interested in a given subject and capable of evaluating the significance of various sources. A teacher, as the holder of complete knowledge on a subject, who dispenses information to students and requires them to master it is increasingly difficult to maintain. This "democratizing" trend is further strengthened wherever new media are present in establishing, maintaining and setting limits on relations. While it is hard to imagine a school successfully operating without a hierarchical model, it is equally hard to ignore that the boundaries of this model are shifting. Divisions between what is public and private are becoming blurred, informal student-teacher communications are on the rise, and a new model of knowledge, largely perceived as being antagonistic to the one currently in place, is entering the educational environment through the back doors.

On a more general level, this poses a question. Are new media being more efficiently and beneficially assimilated in areas which are secondary to the essence of educational institutions? These secondary areas include student-teacher relations and organizational and administrative functions. The schools we saw differed both in terms of "digital development" as well as their uses of technologies. This is a result of the fact that the presence of media in these spheres and the way in which it is used, it is dependent on bottom-up initiatives and unplanned ideas by both teachers and students. The final shape of these media mediations is emerging in mutual negotiations of "figuring out" practices which play out between teachers and students. Due to this digital independence, which exists alongside the official institutions, both sides appreciate the opportunities and challenges created by technology.

Many more tensions and conflicts are emerging among activities directly related to the primary purpose of schools: the organization of access to knowledge and the verification of the results of this knowledge transferral. In this area, both students and teachers' attitudes are not unambiguous. Our young collaborators, even though they frequently viewed online sources of knowledge as being "second-best" compared to textbooks, relied on them in their everyday practices. This reliance manifested itself both in skillfully processing information which they gathered online, to simply copying and pasting "ready-made" sources or even using mobile phones to cheat in class (cheating is especially prevalent in subjects deemed uninteresting or too difficult). Teachers, who are the representatives of educational institutions, were mostly skeptical about content which students gathered online. While they find organizational and communication uses of the internet to be valuable, the online world as a source of knowledge was viewed negatively. Unless, of course, the online content was posted directly by the teachers, allowing them a measure of control over this process. Despite the spectrum of student and teacher attitudes, the internet is a presence which significantly affects the learning process – creating confusion among both sides. It is in this area, that a lack of systemic solutions is most clearly felt. Such solutions would help ensure that the online world created more opportunities than dangers in the school-based educational process.

Schools and new media

It is impossible for schools to become institutions that are tightly woven together with cultural experiences. However, even if centralized school planning documents suggest otherwise, schools have already changed – claims **Tomasz Szkudlarek**, a pedagogue from the University of Gdańsk

"New media" are overwhelmingly a challenge to the way in which schools function, they raise questions as to the institution's social aims. Of course, there are previous examples of this process. In the 1960s, long before the rise of the internet, Ivan Illich wrote about a utopian "society without schools." In it, education was to be based on self-education networks. Illich's utopia is now, to a large extent, here, and some of the educational initiatives undertaken by the European Union (for example, certificates for skills gained outside formal educational systems) are clearly bringing us closer to containing it within some systemic boundaries. In this sense, the redefining of the idea of school is already taking place. To a large extent, policies on educational content and examination – without the associated changes in systemic self-awareness – has already changed its goals, while still using ideologies which mask it (such as, "society of knowledge"). School has already changed – it performs functions that differ from those outlined in the central program documents. However, the separation between "school" and "world" as experienced by the teenagers in this report cannot be eliminated – it is an endemic difference, with deep historical, political and cultural roots. It stems from schools' origins – connected, at first, with the Church, later, with political visions of public enlightenment and lastly with the nation-state. In all of these arrangements, schools were designed to act "against" the social world, as an institution working toward a "nonexistent" world. Even today's ideologies such as globalization or knowledge society have a similar, otherworldly character – they insist on a certain logic of school function which is not necessarily based on common experiences outside of it. This separation of school and world has two dimensions: the conservative one (school as an institution which transfers culture, a machine creating group identities based on mass myths, histories or rationalities – a world which "no longer" exists) and a radical one (school as an institution which shapes the future, utopian – a world which does not "yet" exist). These dimensions are entangled with a measure of direct, "here and now" adjustment to modernity. There does not seem to be a chance for schools to become institutions which are wholly intertwined with the cultural experience, as that would mean the end of education and a return to original cultural forms, the transferral of which would be based on socialization. In the "Foresight" program, I am attempting to pose the hypothesis that adaptive dimension of education, which involves a broader opening to the non-school world, a more practical approach suffused in modern educational technologies and their pop-culture equivalents, could see a massive blossoming in public schools. Private schools – due to education's segregationist functions, which are a key element of the re-creation of a class structure within Polish society – will, in my mind, become distinctly conservative.

People always have, and always will, function between in-school and out-of-school learning. This is the only viable way of looking at educational institutions. School will never be able to completely dominate learning, and it was never designed to do so. The efforts of schools are simply "another text" introduced into the sphere of social experiences – and it can become significant only when it undergoes a process of "updating" in the second dimension which I mentioned. This point is capably illustrated by the examples of engaged teachers who maintain good contact with their students – without these types of teachers one can still live actively, but when their actions connect with out-of-school experiences, we can see a certain added effect. We can hope that it will be further developed thanks to the increasing popularity of networked thinking, which includes schools in varied forms of social partnership. However, I caution against overestimating the influence of new communication methods on school institutions. We must keep in mind that "technological revolutions" in schools, starting with television in 1960s United States, have generally had a very small influence on their primary educational content. These innovations are usually introduced due to economic reasons (it will be cheaper), later, pedagogical underpinnings are introduced (such as with distance learning where non-synchronized communication allowed for flexible scheduling), and finally we discover that the new is an updating of the old (after all, distance learning is simply a newer version of correspondence courses). That's when we can realistically evaluate the innovation's strengths and weaknesses, and with a lowered enthusiasm we can note that "nothing can replace in-person contact." Another matter, are built-in competency barriers: children are usually more adept at using these technologies than adults (back in the 1960s, Margaret Mead wrote about "reversed" intergenerational teaching), and non-school institutions are more adept than school ones. According to our studies, computer science students in their third year and later, who usually work at high technology companies, introduce their universities to technologies that are newer than the ones available in the academic world. In this context, the digital competencies of many of high school students who participated in this report were not very impressive. Perhaps young people no longer see these technologies as new and exciting?

In the report we can read about instances of decreasing distance between teachers and students. This decreasing distance, which many teachers are comfortable with, frequently occurs over social networks, and internet communicators, which is not a new phenomenon. Perhaps an equally valid theory would be that students used to have much more knowledge about their teachers' private lives (and the reverse). The observations regarding increasingly group-work focused students seem particularly accurate – of course, school-age individualism is frequently a fiction. This individual optic (which is still being contested by students) is not the school's shortcoming or even invention. It was imposed on it by the current social order. Educational traditions contain many group-work experiences and conceptions (working on projects has been known to educators for over 100 years) and is still a part of pedagogical instruction. We could very easily bring it back into school practices, but that would be at odds with the logic of examinations, with neoliberal individualism which claims that competition between individuals is necessary. And, on a deeper and less visible level – with the ideology of a knowledge economy/society, where knowledge is supposed to be "privatized" and closely guarded. In this sense, students who help each other are acting illogically and against their own interests. This is why the more ambitious ones, those more results-oriented, will enter into such cooperative arrangements less frequently; others will probably abandon them at higher levels of education. This problem brings us to an out-of-school network of relationships in this country, to the lack of culturally accepted communal ideologies (such as European social-democracy, or American communitarianism). We are directing all of our energies to bolstering the processes of individualization, privatization and parametrization. Individualism at school is only one of the effects of these processes.

Tomasz Szkudlarek

MAL DU SIÈCLE?

In the smoothly modern world of new media, happenstance has replaced consequence, order has given way to chaos, and time appears to be torn into shreds, chopped into fragments with no past or future and consequence-free episodes – writes **Zygmunt Bauman** in a discussion with **Mateusz Halawa**. How do people gain agency in a world which appears as a database?

Mateusz Halawa: In this report we looked at two phenomena: new communication technologies as unique cultural forms, which promote a certain lifestyle, and people acting within a specific, material environment shaped by these new forms of cultural circulation.

New media theoretician Lev Manovich writes that in the computer era, a new form of culture is emerging – the database. While novels or films (thus, relatively "old" media) favored narration, or the telling of stories by arranging elements into sequences, the computer – one of the fundamental objects in the lives of our collaborators – advances an entirely different principle. "Many new media objects do not tell stories; they do not have beginning or end; in fact, they don't have any development, thematically, formally or otherwise which would organize their elements into a sequence. Instead, they are collections of individual items, where every item has the same significance as any other." (Manovich 2001: 218).

One of the fundamental experiences shared by our collaborators is using a computer. Whether it means using Wikipedia to answer a physics problem, or using communicators to stay in intimate contact with a loved one after separating physically, or looking at a friend's blog to see and comment on photos from a night out on the town, all of it appears to be significantly different from experiences with older media. Manovich suggests that these experiences represent a new model of the world's structure. For computer users, he writes, "the world appears to us as an endless and unstructured collection of images, texts, and other data records." (Manovich, 2001: 219). We are tempted to follow this insight. The findings of our ethnographers seem to confirm this interpretation, as they describe social practices which are not "just" reading or looking, but also (maybe even primarily) navigating, searching, creating connections, copying and reconfiguring.

"As a cultural form," Manovich writes, "the database represents the world as a list of items and it refuses to order this list. In contrast, a narrative creates a cause-and-effect trajectory of seemingly unordered items (events). Therefore, database and narrative are natural enemies. Competing for the same territory of human culture, each claims an exclusive right to make meaning out of the world" (2001: 225).

I am interested in looking at this proposition from the point of view of people inhabiting this world which appears as a database. What can crafting the "self" and making life significant mean in a cultural environment which, structurally, is a collection of possible elements, and not a cohesive narrative, or even a collection of cohesive narratives?

Zygmunt Bauman: From Socrates to Freud – as J.M. Coetzee reminds us in an essay about the Italian writer Aron Ettore Schmitz, better known as Italo Svevo, Western moral philosophy espoused the Delphic credo "know thyself!" But, if one trusts Schopenhauer's opinion (as Svevo did), that human character is based on will and that it is doubtful that will would want to abandon its desires – what good can "knowing thyself" be? It could only make a human suffer, cause a split in personality, suffering, despair at the cruel fate and personal helplessness, and thrashing about in a snare. The will, like the voice which spoke to Moses on Mount Sinai, cannot stand to be questioned, much less be asked for its reason for existence; its lofty "I am that I am" does not invite discussion – it ends it before it even begins. The will would not be itself if it acted any other way. Will is a declaration of the impossibility to refuse (as Kafka noted, a flock of circling and cawing crows seems like it could peck heaven apart; but as he quickly adds: heaven simply means: the impossibility of crows).

Being born of will, and drawing its power and impudence from it, character – it seems, could not be at odds with will. At least, that's what logic would suggest. But, despite logic, which as we know, is based on the logic of in-disputability, the will is both character's armor and a caustic acid eating away at it. Character calls on the will both in moments when it's struggling for its existence (honor, loyalty to principles, consistency, self-respect), as well as when it dreams of being different than it is (self development, promotion, cleansing of pollution, a new start). Zeno Cosini, the protagonist of Svevo's last novel, becomes terrified of the will's Gorgon-like stare, when both of her Janus-like faces look at him at the same time, he falls ill, and simultaneously wants and does not want to be cured. Effort is of no help here, neither is the advice of Freudian therapists to treat the festering wound of split personality with the soothing elixir of self-knowledge. As Coetzee claims, we are not dealing with a defect of Zeno's ego (if it wasn't for his publisher's concern about the title's effect on sales, Svevo's first novel was to be known as *L'Inetto* – Klutz, Ass, Loser, Dud or to use more direct language a Bungler or an Oaf) but rather with the fact that there's too much power for only a solitary self. We're talking about the *mal du siècle*, the internal splitting of European civilization, whose common weakness cannot be cured with any quantity of the concoction used to glue together each separated self.

Modern civilization's native illness is based on the idea/plan/promise of uniting water and fire: the reconciling of the safety of *being yourself* with the freedom to become *someone else*. As this dual, internally contradictory reason for waging war on the existing state of affairs is as impossible to accomplish as transforming the cauldron of eternally feuding Afghan tribes into a parliamentary democracy – the plan cannot succeed, and the promise can never be fulfilled. Given the lack of any chances for lasting peace we can only expect an unending stream of skirmishes, interrupted by temporary and tenuous cease fires. Each skirmish does not bring us closer to the end of the war, and each cease fire does not bring us closer to a peace treaty. The effort to reconcile the solidity of existence with an ease of reincarnation has been transformed, despite our hopes, from a one-time and irreversible action into an unending chase after the fleeting horizon. As well as from the promise of a top-down and *wholesale* resolution to the matter – through the creation of a social order which is optimally suited to achieving the goal, into a call to resolve matters on a *retail* level – through finding ploys and tricks which optimally fit the goal.

As a result of this double transformation of the "modern project," the passage of experienced time has turned into movement without a set direction (similar to "Brownian motion" in elementary physics – the liquid is full of flashes and eruptions but it does not move). Chance has replaced consistency, a set of accidental circumstances replaced determination, order has given way to chaos – time has scattered like beads from a broken rosary. *Lebenszeit* – lifetime – is not cyclical; it is not a series of nomadic returns or the trail of a pilgrim's voyage. The new *Lebenszeit*, in a manner of speaking, is pointillistic: as each one of the attempts to reconcile the authenticity of existence with the temptation/need for its constant transformation is doomed to failure, the distance between the start and abandonment of each ensuing effort shortens, eventually becoming the size of a point (a figure which, paradoxically, lacks size under the rules of geometry). The frequency of interruptions in continuity is meant to compensate the inherent tendency toward disintegration and painful faults of each one of the versions of the state, which currently (but for how long?) lay claim to permanence.

As Marshall McLuhan noted at the beginning of the electronic revolution: the medium is the message. This is in direct contrast to the offline world, where (as Nietzsche ordered Zarathustra to prophetically proclaim) the past, with its petrified settlements must become a nightmare where we "gnash [our] teeth and curse." In the online world, a world conveyed (revealed? constructed? simulated?) by electronic media, time appears to be torn to shreds, chopped into fragments without a history or a future and episodes without a consequence; the sequence of events can be freely changed without harm to (the inherently self-sufficient) sense of the revealed episodes, and the cutting of each one of them is as simple and instantaneous as calling them into (inherently fleeting) life. Nothing here is forever, nothing has to leave indelible traces behind or remains which cannot be cleaned up: the "delete" key takes care of that. The lack of this "delete" key in the offline reality becomes increasingly frustrating, causing the online world to win all its beauty, comfort, and appeal contests with the offline one. Media no longer have to seek fidelity to realities of life; it is the realities of life which must resemble visual media and try to match their advantages. The decision to abandon this competition can only result in their demise.

"Reconciling the safety of *being yourself* with the freedom to become *someone else*" – the task set before itself and promised by the brash modern spirit – appears to be as hopeless as squaring the circle. It is, and probably will remain so – as far as the offline world is concerned. The online world, on the other hand, offers both, but, in the process, cheapens these two values, the reconciliation of which modern life promised. The online sense of "safety" may not be able to survive the transfer into the more severe and colder climate of offline life; and the happiness drawn from "freedom," drawn from the ease of assuming new identities in the closed spaces of the online world, may not be able to survive the shedding of these costumes which are tolerated (with a wink) only during carnival.

Of course, online natives might not be able to recognize this. They've become used to noticing the things which the electronic world brought into focus and have forgotten to look for things which did not find a place in the fragmented, episodo-puentellist online world.

Mateusz Halawa: This episodic and fragmented world which appears as a database creates, as you wrote, a unique temporal regime. The chopped, fragmented *Lebenszeit* appears as a place where creating durability, continuity and cohesiveness appear to be doomed to failure.

Try to understand: if there is one defining feature of the brains of people my age, it is a fucked up chronology; first the word 'first' leaves our heads. Then, the word 'then.' Next, the word 'next.' Phrases like – And then he, At that moment, At the same time, Three days later. Despite it all, each one of these stories has a Now point. A point, from which you can determine and arrange all events. [...] **Time is compost. Events are scattered papers. Flashcards.** (Jakub Żulczyk, Radio Armageddon, 2008, p. 5-6)

And still, we try to put together this world which has fallen apart, put it together into a whole. The reports of our researchers describe various social practices, but many of them are connected: they can be interpreted as community-building practices, putting together a whole, creating cause-effect narratives from what appears to be an archive of scattered elements. **The world may have gotten fragmented, but we're still trying to have selfhood in it. We're talking about selfhood as something achieved through hard work, and not just as a given. This work of uniting the scattered, engages a multitude of technologies in the lives of our collaborators, sometimes in a paradoxical ways. Mobile phones – one of the technologies of modern individualism – are being used in attempts to foster bonds and create proximity. The global internet is (as the co-internet) used to create or recreate a sense of locality, which was shaken by the processes of globalization which were fueled by the rise of the internet.** I'm not sure if the on and offline worlds are clearly distinguishable.

Your writings about changes in the social perception of time, shed an interesting light on our team's discussions about "Youth and media." We were struck by how much of the content created by our collaborators – photos from parties, blog entries, Nasza-klasa comments – are suffused with nostalgia. (The participants were 17 and 18 years old.) New media allow the transformation of ongoing events into artifacts of the "past," which can be manipulated by immediately creating memories, telling of stories, and constructing narratives from them. This longing for a time that has not yet ended – Frederic Jameson writes of a nostalgia for the present – infuses many of the practices we studied. It appears that the experience of life in the pointillistic time of new media, is often connected to the sense of loss. Nostalgia is now becoming one of the primary structures of experiencing.

Zygmunt Bauman: Each point in pointillistic time is the present. In order for it to go beyond the present, it would have to be "impregnated" – made pregnant with consequences which would outlive it: a future. And, we all desire such an impregnation – we are all infected with this type of libido. But, as we get started, we immediately recall that you can not be a little pregnant; and removing the fetus is connected to significant, unpleasant problems. Impregnating a moment with a future makes one a hostage of a notoriously capricious fate. So, as was the case with Cosini, we both want and do not want, desire and fear ... the internet's guarantee of abortion on demand (we can take advantage of it or not, we'll see in some ensuing present) provided at the time of conception provides us with a solution to the dilemma, a solution which in Cosini's situation of being sentenced to a world (which due to a lack of an alternative was not yet called "offline") where it was not only unavailable but even inconceivable.

From this standpoint, it is easier and seemingly safer, to provide the present with a *past* of which pointillistic time robbed it. After all, the past has already happened, and thus is naturally resistant to the caprices of fate. We immediately know what parts of it we choose, and which we reject – as with any trip to the supermarket or online store. But nostalgia is born of the desire to nail down the uppity *future*, out of fear of an orphan's fate, or the humiliation of a foundling... Binding the future with a nostalgic cement can turn out to be only a seemingly safe undertaking. Fate, which is incurably fickle, can instantaneously change a past that was recalled from nonexistence and settled in the current and future present from a safe harbor into a prison cell. Isn't it thus better to travel "light," able, if need arises, to hop the prison walls in a single leap? Traveling with no baggage, with just a cellphone and a laptop, because any additional package, no matter how valuable, can become a terrible ballast following yet another turn of fate? Thus, we go back to Cosini. I'd want to, he explained, but I'm afraid.

Your accurate observations suppose the existence of an *Eindeutigkeit* – an unambiguity – which our existence in a liquid-modern world and the art of constructing self-existence in it, does not and could not, posses. As far as I can, I try not to pass value judgements on choices people make when facing dilemmas. I stubbornly insist that life in the liquid-modern world forces choices, that it is a string of dilemmas which only have *compromise and halfhearted* solutions, never *perfect* ones. These dilemma's are all too real, and we cannot be surprised that individuals entering this world struggle with solving them, and by trial and error ("hard work" as you described it) establish the location of traps and snares that this world is full of. *Mal du siècle*, as Coetzee termed it, and I insist on repeating.

Finally, you are right in highlighting that "we're still trying to have selfhood" in this world. I would add, that it does not seem as if we will ever stop trying. (I would also add that we have selfhood in our individualized world on the basis of history's decree; these attempts which you are describing, are efforts aimed at transforming "selfhood *de jure*" into "selfhood *de facto.*") To paraphrase Marx, I would also say that people build their selves in an environment not of their construction, using the resources and construction technology which they find at the construction site, while digging the foundations. It is an inventory of available building materials and technologies which makes some human choices more probable than others (assuming, of course, that we're talking about rational beings with good intentions!). I believe that as cultural researchers, we should focus on the qualities of these building materials and technologies, on their positives and negatives, their capabilities and limits – to help people "attempt to establish selfhood" with conscious knowledge of the realities... That might be the most useful of services, which we can offer the audience of our work.

Zygmunt Bauman

NEW QUESTIONS ABOUT CULTURAL PARTICIPATION

Changes in cultural environment related to the development of new media described in this report demand a new vocabulary to discuss "cultural participation." old categories, such as "consumer," are becoming problematic at a time when people are drawn into the processes of co-creating and distributing cultural content, frequently outside of the system of institutions. How should we think of cultural participation when the old categories have become obsolete?

Żuku: no longer a consumer, not yet a creator

One of the most significant problems we faced writing this report, were language limitations relating to the social and cultural changes which are taking place. Some of these changes involve the blurring of boundaries between production and consumption. While it appears that a strict division between producers and consumers cannot be maintained (evidenced by the portmanteau "prosumer"), we still lack the appropriate vocabulary to capture all of the shades in between. In a world where media objects' business plans, as well as communication architecture which distributes and redistributes these objects, put a premium on active consumers, we cannot interpret every mouse click and online interaction as a creative gesture. Some of these actions are of a trivial nature, such as copying music for a friend or sending a link to a Rapidshare file which they can download themselves. Often, the boundary between the trivial and non-trivial escapes clear classification – after all, contributing to an online music forum can, but does not have to be a meaningful action which translates into group attention to particular content (for example, recommending an unknown artist to a group). The issue is particularly important, since most of the teenagers we met did not create or remix music. However, in a culture of abundance, where the problem is no longer availability of content, but rather knowledge which items are worth choosing, individuals who filter and catalogue freely available content are no less important than those who create it. Because, if you can find nearly anything, than what do you look for?

In the pre-internet era of scarcity, social networks for exchanging music were limited by the physicality of the carriers of cultural content and were based on transferring recordings. In those circumstances, the value of knowledge was much lower because knowing the a particular band plays good music did not bring the audience closer to hearing it. Today is different. Frequently, mp3 music files are attached to the knowledge itself. The role of recordings has been degraded – dozens of albums can be crammed onto a single DVD disc which is burned in 10 minutes, and hundreds of links to download sites appear after a simple web search – content alone has become less significant. Knowledge which content is interesting is truly valued. With this knowledge, the content is easily reachable, and if a lack of competencies is an obstacle, a friend can always download an album and bring it to school the next day. One such person is Żuku, a Metallica fan. Music is his biggest passion. He is enthusiastic about finding new music online and, unlike a brief stint as a guitarist in a local band, this hobby does not seem to be exhausting itself. Żuku's future plans include music – he hopes to be a music journalist. If we assume that a music journalist is a person who helps others find artists who are of interest to them, he already is one.

Much of Żuku's music activity is tied to his favorite band. Thanks to the internet he has an impressive collection of Metallica recordings – about 11,000 in total. *I have all the studio and live albums, I have all of their demos, all their singles and EPs, all instrumental tracks, I have recordings of their rehearsals, I do not have all the bootlegs yet, so far about 500 from 1982 to 1996. I still have a list of links to 1300 concerts, and I want to download them all,* he says. Typical of the teenagers we met during our research, Żuku does not think of his actions as piracy. He focuses on the joy attached to searching for and sharing music with friends who always know that he'll gladly burn them an album they want. At the same time, as he explains, *I'll throw in something that I'm into, and think they might be interested in as well.* Żuku is thus a connoisseur, and an expert who spends much time developing his knowledge of music, and freely shares it with his friends. Music, while an intimate matter, is also an element of sociability and a part of the system of gift exchanges – Żuku's friends do not worry about a lack of new music, while he gains increased respect in their eyes. His main benefit is the satisfaction and acknowledgment, which does not change the fact that he often brings an external hard drive with him when visiting friends. After all, sharing music and movies is as much of a part of friendship as talking about them. Of course, exchanging music played similar roles in the lives of older generations, but Żuku's parents did not have the ability to listen to dozens of new albums a month. To Żuku and his peers, the internet is an endless source of free music, and an ever-growing encyclopedia of music reviews and recommendations. It is an encyclopedia in which Żuku wrote a few articles himself, being active on an online Metallica forum. This forum is a place to exchange knowledge, but also music itself: *When somebody asks me for something on the forum, then I'll usually send them a link to rapidshare, and add in some bonuses from myself. Then I get a "huge thanks, buddy," and I reply "no problem, I'll be in touch when I'll need something.* Sometimes, it allows him to make new friends – also online. His activity on the forum is the basis of relationships which allow him to have a free place to stay anytime he goes anywhere in Poland for a concert.

Henry Jenkins: new forms of cultural participation

A world in which consumers help shape networked media circulation of content, is entirely different from the one in which consumers passively received content provided by distribution channels.
It appears that young people today perceive themselves and their roles in contacts with media differently than older generations – claims **Henry Jenkins**, a media studies scholar at the university of southern california in a conversation with **Mirosław Filiciak**.

Mirosław Filiciak: In your book, *Convergence Culture* (Jenkins, 2006), you describe the new cultural elites developing in a digital media environment. Fans actively transform official cultural texts, create remixes and their own works inspired by pop culture. Their art, once restricted to cultural margins, is more and more frequently collaborating or even competing with commercial producers, thanks to powerful and free distribution channels.

The young people we met during our study, may seem not to be *as* productive in creating content. At the same time, they cannot simply be referred to as passive consumers. In fact, many of them are *bona fide* pop culture experts, who actively co-create culture, spreading and commenting on its contents. Their competencies, while frequently directed at a single niche, are surprisingly well developed, and sharing their media collections is one of the key elements of their lives. This is the case with Żuku, whose hard drive contains 11,000 mp3s of Metallica songs.

We've found that it is very difficult to separate our collaborators' social relations from their cultural activities – as digital media make not only copying easier, but also enhance sharing within peer networks. We're wondering how to describe this grey area located somewhere between creativity and consumption?

Henry Jenkins: Some of our first attempts to characterize the new participatory culture have pointed attention on exceptional cases -- the most active, creative, and visible sectors of fandom, for example. Yet, the changes being wrought by participatory culture are often more subtle and may extend to much more mundane and everyday new media practices. For example, my work on spreadable media focuses on small, local decisions to pass along content from one user to the other, often with fairly simple tags or messages. These individual decisions to circulate content collectively have a strong impact on the contemporary mediascape -- certain content becomes visible, others drops from our attention, as result of these fairly modest forms of participation. A world where consumers help to shape the flow of media across networks is a very different realm than one where we passively accept what is offered to us via broadcast channels. All signs are that young people see themselves and their role in media differently -- they know that they have the potential to make much more visible contributions -- as a result of these modest and peripheral forms of participation.

Mirosław Filiciak: What challenges does this new media-fueled cultural environment pose to cultural institutions?

Henry Jenkins: From an educational point of view, these forms of participations may allow them to acquire new technical and social skills, may motivate them to deepen their expertise, and may empower them to speak with greater confidence about what they know. These localized practices may at the same time heighten civic awareness as they feel a greater sense of connection to others in their social networks and as they come away with a sense that they have something valuable to contribute to the conversations of their community.

Wiesław Godzic: television's end, creativity's beginning

Couches in front of tv sets have emptied, tv sets are gradually losing their status as critical furniture. We are witnessing the spread of new models of cultural consumption which are distinguished by a desire to abandon traditional television's limits. At the same time, we still have not developed metaphors which could describe this situation – writes **Wiesław Godzic**, a media studies expert at the university of social sciences and humanities in warsaw. Is the tv viewer no longer the paradigm of a consumer of culture?

Media are divided into those whose consumption demands leaving home and going to a place where they are being broadcast or performed, and those which are easily domesticated and can be taken in during meals, vacuuming or tinkering at home. Theatre, light and sound shows, films and television in public places – are examples of the first category. On the other hand, most of television and the majority of newer electronic media belong to a category which does not require a sport coat and styled hair before entering into the public sphere – all of them take place at home, in a safe space.

This clear, 20th century division is experiencing a series of disturbances which makes it worthwhile to consider the spot we are currently in. In *Home Territories: Media, Mobility and Identity*, British media sociologist David Morley noted this as a moment of the blurring of boundaries between two – up to now separate spheres (Morley, 2003). When I consider Morely's presentation of exotic examples of multi-cultural media use in Great Britain, I am noticing a very similar situation occurring in Poland. In fact, I believe that what is happening in Poland is even more dramatic, as ethnic cultural boundaries seem to be playing an ever-smaller role in the consumption of audiovisual content – and members of cultures such as Poland's, which entered onto this path relatively late (for various reasons), are expanding a lot of effort to catch up to the norms which until recently were mocked. An analysis of television station viewership shows how deep this stratification of television audiences can become. This seems obvious, as "obvious" as the results of the research presented here. In my mind their clarity and unambiguity is superficial: they are actually intriguing enough to merit a multifaceted discussion.

In my opinion, the most interesting finding resulting from the observation of media usage by participants in the "Youth and Media" project, deals with a change in distribution channels of television shows and, the related **gradual, but persistent decline of the TV set as a piece of furniture, as a separate device.** It isn't that the television is disappearing for young modern Poles – that will take time – but it is becoming on of many large streams of sounds and images which enter the home, school, cafe, anywhere. As this content is varied – there is a need for a device which will integrate them into a single stream.

It is interesting to consider that this new media situation has not developed a common metaphor which would be able to describe and explain the state of consumption. Historically, since the 1940s when television entered into the territory of the radio medium. I remember a quaint British postcard of a common room – which in British houses used to be the dining room. A grandmother was watching a grandchild: reading a fairytale to him, looking at the illustrations together. The room was cluttered with books, and on top of the chest of drawers was a large radio set. It appeared as if the sound of the radio did not interfere, nor enhance the reading – in a word it did not require any special attention. Nobody in the room is paying attention to the device. A second image comes to mind, this one from 1950s United States. A mother is preparing two kids, eleven or twelve year olds, for school. The boys are eating breakfast, but their attention is fixed on a giant TV set: they're sitting on the floor, very close to the screen and their eyes are fixed on some unidentifiable show's host. Television is an entirely different medium from radio because it requires a different type of attention from its viewers – to describe this means finding a good metaphor which would depict most contact with television during the "pre-internet" era. Even when this metaphor of an "attention catcher" is attached to extreme ideas (for example the cover of Neil Postman's *Amusing ourselves to death* shows tightly packed headless corpses crowded in front of a TV set).

At this point, the series of blunt, accurate, or entirely unwise metaphors which attempted to visualize the process of watching television comes to an end. It would be interesting to show how the television couch began to be abandoned, despite ever-larger and impressive TV sets. When David Morley was describing the art of negotiations surrounding the choosing of a channel to be watched by a family, the transcripts also reflected our 1990s Polish skirmishes. The remote control was truly an attribute of power and control over this process. That era is coming to end – and the research notes in this report show that it is doing so slowly, and even beautifully. But, the problems with metaphors will remain. How do you visualize the superficially accurate slogan "Everyone is playing alone?" Showing an internet user in front of a screen as a lonely nomad in an informational desert (the method used by the authors of a public service poster warning parents and children about the dangers of online relationships). The poster shows a disgusting middle age fat man pretending to be a 12 year old boy. The slogan is, after all, only seemingly accurate, as most modern online interactions – as seen in "Youth and Media" – are an extension of offline social activities. **Will the computer monitor (more and more frequently, a laptop screen, and very soon, a smartphone display) replace the TV screen? Everything points to yes,** or at least the logic of miniaturization and the principle of freedom of content do so. However, as I've mentioned, this will not happen very quickly, and will be kept within certain norms. One of the key principles in this area states that media shift to forms which better fulfill desires, and match the realities of new consumers. This is why, I believe, young people will continue to treat television and its stream of sounds and images as a well-liked piece of junk in which anyone can find something interesting. Discovering a show can still take place accidentally, as if a revelation, but the show's entire series history will be found online, while current episodes could be watched on TV. A similar interest can be directed to niche shows, which can become tools of discovering the past and distant history.

I do not think that interest in television will be the dominant tendency among young consumers of audiovisual content in the upcoming years. It would be interesting to know what broadcasters could/should do to reverse this trend? Perhaps they could provide the type of shows which aren't available online. While it sounds like heresy (one high school student interviewed for this report said that *everything's online)*, I would guess that television could win due to the quality of its programming. Even so, for the young people described in this report, television is not a distribution channel but rather particular audiovisual content which can grab their interest and attention for any number of reasons. They are detaching this product from the traditional consumption scenario characterized by watching at home, usually with several people, with the ability to comment on the show throughout. For the young, such a detaching is a natural phenomenon, while the older generation views it as a revolutionary change.

Thus we are at an in-between stage when it comes to consumption scenarios: on one hand, this is no longer traditional television, but it is also not some new permanent means of dealing with media. Its most important feature, as described in this report, is the desire for freedom, especially creative freedom. A broad range of various manifestations of this desire can be observed. The idea of "time shifting" or watching audiovisual content after its broadcast, with a delay that suits the viewers' schedule. Technology itself is promoting this behavior: modern televisions and satellite tuners have hard drives which allow a user to record a favorite show with one press of a button or to rewind a 'live' broadcast. Further, many broadcasters are aware of this trend and post important content on their own websites minutes after it is broadcast on television. As a last resort, we have portals such as YouTube, a virtual online cinema and television set. In this enormous free film library, we can search for both a past episode of a news magazine and a friend's digital movie – and all of it has been freed from the pressures of schedules and fixed start times.

I think that we are less and less able to recognize this type of freedom – even though it is extremely significant. Watching television used to be connected with a ritual, in which the broadcaster was able to control transmission and content. The ritual has fallen into ruin, as we can watch whenever and with whoever. On the other hand, the other type of creativity is hardly seen in this report. The consumer creates additional communications – they are generally done outside of the artistic society's control and lack any other societal restrictions. The creator–producer has all the tools within reach, all he needs are ideas, desire and a welcoming environment. It will all come – whether we want it or not.

The last phenomenon is least worrisome. It just isn't true that "everyone is playing alone" in the new media world. There are powerful communities grouped around social networking portals and fan groups: it is not surprising that a high school student is convinced that a link she sent will be met with a strong reaction from her friend who is already familiar with this content and has developed his own opinion about it (thanks to others' shared opinions). The informational function is clearly declining, as all of us has the same access to facts. What is strengthening is the function of creating meanings, attaching contexts, or, in other words, pastiching or physically altering content. Television of the future will be a domain of its consumers' creativity. But not for a while, "couch potatoes" will not disappear for many years.

Wiesław Godzic

Wojciech J. Burszta: describing a revolution

We are witnessing the creation of identities which are always open to new propositions and willing to incorporate any available content (both experienced personally as well as through media), as long as it can, temporarily or "conditionally" create a coherent whole. These identities, however, simultaneously incorporate and delete content, and are thus in a constant state of construction and destruction – writes **Wojciech J. Burszta,** a cultural studies expert and co-author of a report on polish urban culture.

A team led by Barbara Fatyga and me, conducted studies in 2008 regarding the state of Polish urban culture (Burszta, Fatyga et al, 2010). Our report showed the scale of the massive changes which are occurring within the cultural sphere and the challenges faced in any analysis of them. There is an inadequacy of most existing analytical terms (culture, free time, cultural activity, cultural identity, cultural canons, cultural participation) used by theoreticians and those actively involved in "cultural policy."

The need to unmask various myths, stereotypes, and simplifications which surround today's cultural discourse is a pressing matter. We are witnessing a cultural revolution: changes are affecting both cultural participation as well as the cultural environment itself. In our report on urban culture we described, among others, the so-called transportation culture best depicted by commuters whose headphone-clad heads are directed toward overhead monitors, or buried in books or newspapers on the Warsaw metro or commuter rail cars.

An "insert" identity

One of the common themes of these changes is the decreasing significance of cultural institutions. Various analyses of Polish cultural institutions show that an increasing number of people in managerial roles are aware of this trend, and are attempting to fight it through rapid modernization. The immediate effects of this process can be seen in the growing number of so-called prosumers – individuals who are both creators and consumers of culture. This evolution beyond passive consumption is the *de facto* norm among the youngest generation – which is described on the adjoining pages of the "Youth and Media" report. I've described this new situation with the phrase: "insert" identities.

The common availability of media allows individuals to distance themselves from their surrounding "local culture," which can result in increased creativity. Still, both the "self" and life within a global ecumenist imagination is subject to availability of media content, over which people lack control. In other words, we are dealing with a paradox of reflexivity (stemming from individualization) and dependency (stemming from institutionalization). This is why we can say that we are witnessing the creation of an identity which can be referred to as an "insert" identity. These identities are always open to new propositions and willing to incorporate any available content (both personally experienced as well as through media), as long as it can, temporarily and "conditionally," create a coherent whole. These identities, however, simultaneously incorporate and delete content, and are thus in a constant state of construction and destruction.

"Insert" identities perfectly reflect the changing model of cultural participation – lacking traditional institutional ties, remediated by media and characterized by a constantly changing offer and an ever-deepening short-term character of accepted values. The results of all the studies conducted by Barbara Fatyga and me show that this is actually happening. This is why it is worth examining the very model of cultural experience. The model referred to by Andrzej Ziemilski as "continuous revealing of culture" is clearly on the defensive. This model of experiencing the world "through culture," is mediated by literature and interpreted through the use of artistic categories. In it, cultural experiences have a specialized character and include familiarity with the canons of artistically-aesthetic "high culture" literature. Today, when this type of writing is largely limited to niche status, the role of professionals and other active participants in literary culture (which was so significant during Poland's communist era) is dying. Most Poles are adamant that they make their own choices in this field, based on personal preferences and identifications with specific genres of literature (mostly popular and/or historical).

Ziemilski described the other model of cultural experience as "culture dominated by praxis," and it describes most participants in cultural life. It is marked by a non-systematic knowledge of artistic works of varying levels (based on traditional evaluative criteria) which provide meaningful aesthetic experiences and elements which develop individual artistic-aesthetic competences. The entirety of factual knowledge and competencies does not result in a cohesive, specific whole, it is rather an element of the "insert" identity. This model of cultural experience, while not in decline, makes up only a part of a larger cultural competence, within which traditional literature and written culture are relegated to a lower status.

The third model of cultural experiences is unequivocally connected with mass and electronic media. In the 1980s, when Zamilski developed his theories, this model was only beginning to appear in Polish culture. Now, it is dominant. We participate in culture through media, and this participation is mostly limed to obtaining information about culture, it is, as described by Alfred Schütz a type of, "accessible knowledge" which allows a basic awareness in the field of artistic cultural participation. The individuals we studied, have a broad awareness of "what's going on" in culture, which does not mean that they take advantage of available cultural offerings (a withdrawal from culture, explained by the "lack of free time").

Culture as relations with content, not institutions

In the current situation, most traditional cultural institutions have no chance for survival. The changes in forms of participation, driven by technology and civilizational changes, are essentially irreversible. Further, Poland has not yet completed the process of systemic change in social and economic spheres, as well as in narrowly-defined cultural ones. A complete rebuilding of a system made up of nearly 40 million people cannot be accomplished within twenty years. We are witnessing significant confusion in the cultural sphere: unstable characteristics and profiles of consumers of culture, chaotic institutions, disorganization of time and the structure of everyday life, as well as changes in the function and character of cultural activities. Finally, we are seeing deep changes in cultural awareness and discourses surrounding it.

The theses presented here are based on observations made during work on the report on Polish urban culture. However, they are largely confirmed by the observations made among teenagers during the creation of this report – especially in their views on cultural participation. While the method of selecting research subjects was different in both reports, we can clearly see two emerging trends. First, a shift away from traditionally structured cultural institutions in favor of creating cultural communities which function "like" institutions, such as YouTube. These new institutions function without input from government and state actors and official cultural policies. Second, "convergence culture" is embracing ever bigger and popular forms, based mostly on constant monitoring and altering (ironically, creatively, or polemically) official cultural content, including commercial productions. It is also proof of the entrenching of the newness metaculture which states that the essence of the circulation of cultural content today is their proliferation as various content, which reference each other and grow simultaneously creating image and text-basedcompounds of meanings. It appears that no cultural content can claim to be truly autonomous, as it immediately becomes an element of metacultural transformation through all available media – both traditionally cultural and technical ones.

In light of these examples, we must acknowledge that **we are witnessing the explosion of a super-new culture. This revolution primarily affects the cultural identity of young Poles. Identity is becoming more elastic and self-reflexive, more individualized and autonomous of traditional "merging" indicators. Culture is increasingly an area of choices made without reference to any social arrangements, it is not a culture that is identified with institutions but rather with available content, which accompanies people around the clock.** There is no clear canon of culture, even though its rudimentary remains are noticeable in people's choices and reasons for them. In light of the destruction of the two earlier models of cultural experience (continuous revealing of culture and culture as praxis), the third model is becoming ever more significant: ever present, mediated culture which creates "insert" identities. It requires a new model for studying cultural participation and the role of culture, and, most of all, a revision of the understanding of cultural canons (abandoning strict hierarchies and replacing them with realistic categories *in statu nascendi*) and the incorporation of new media cultural products which are completely transforming the cultural experiences of young Poles.

Wojciech J. Burszta

Marek Krajewski: expiration

Young people live in a world that is not so much lacking communities, as it is being ruled by new laws. New media separate their users during processes of receiving and transforming data, but can also unite them in new types of communities. These groups, while scattered and not grounded in the physical world, depend on strong bonds which unite their members. **Marek Krajewski** of Poznań's Adam Mickiewicz University writes about new forms of socialization emerging through new media usage practices.

Modern communication devices are based on restricted codes, which invalidate elaborated codes (I am referring here to the classic differentiation introduced by Basil Bernstein – see Bokszański and others, 1977: 109-113). The language of emails, internet communicators, Facebook, Nasza-klasa, Twitter and forum discussions is primarily subject to the tempo at which information is transferred. It is also related to the capabilities built into the devices themselves (miniaturized, restrictions on character count), and the primary context of their use (usually during other activities, in between, in public spaces). Restricted codes, it is worth noting, are not simply defined by limited means of expression or the tendency toward shortcuts, but, most fundamentally, by contextualization and situationism. These technologies allow us to contact only those that are plugged into our most immediate world, with whom we share our everyday, who watch, read and perceive things similar to our own. The consequence of their use is individuals' dependency on groups. If the individual only uses these restricted codes, than he speaks and thinks in terms of the group's experiences and creations. Since the individual does not posses his own, autonomous points of reference, it is difficult to leave the group behind, as it becomes the fundamental point of reference and provides confidence to act. At the same time, the group forces a de-individualization, obstructs independence and endangers the individual's autonomy. Even though this phenomenon runs counter to Western societies' fetishized cult of individuality (especially its rivalry-driven versions) it appears to be highly functional in face of the new cultural environment in which young people live. The uniqueness of this situation can be described using the term "black box" (see p. 47). Both this situation, and the social human-object hybrids require a simplified code of communications, as only it allows an efficient collaboration between people and machines, and energizes movement and circulation of content – which sustain the network.

The contextuality of restricted codes means that, while we are all connected to the Web, and equally dependent on communication devices, we still form separate human-object communities which generate social divisions (including intergenerational ones). These intergenerational divides are further bolstered through restricted codes' properties, as well as through the uniqueness of remediation devices which are personalized and used idiosyncratically. By this, I do not mean that young people do not use certain types of cellphones because they're "not cool," or that they fetishize some devices as being uniquely "youthful." Mobile phones are a type of device which is frequently individualized by users, who treat this process as equivalent to the development of an individual as a unique person. The means which provide a feeling of uniqueness include wallpapers, ring-tones, screen savers, skins, cases, stickers or key-chains, as well as personalized interface or software. An individual's uniqueness, realized through adaptations of factory design and default software, is not just symbolic but becomes factual. These adaptations lead to specific types of communications, position an individual in the network and result in the utilization of only some of the resources offered by the Web. The first level at which this process takes place is modifying the communication process, defining potential partners based on use of same types of devices, its availability, price, look, or manner of individualizing it (this is the function of colored earphones or a defining of the owner's aesthetic sensibility through phone covers, ringtones, music, and wallpapers on the screen). A communication medium, defined here as an object, communicates in the same way that status symbols always have. It symbolizes its owner's tribal sense of belonging, his aspirations and location on the social map. Here, the object unites and divides not due to its primary communicative function, but rather based on semiotic relations connecting it to various social strata.

A second, much more interesting level is made up of communication modes which are a function of a device's hardware and software specifications, as well as the user's ability to modify them. This second level is the domain of geeks, tech-fans and members of that "scene," and it creates intragenerational divisions based on access to specialized knowledge and competences. These technologies and their related devices, which, as we stated, comprise a new natural environment for the youngest generation, create divisions and subcultures within it, and function on a similar level as differentiated relations with the biological world used to. They reflect a level of its control by the individual and his successful adaptations. That which makes similar (here the common access to communication technologies), as long as it is perceived as nature, must create new divisions, differences and, eventually, inequalities. Media-objects de-individualize, but only on a local and context-driven level, in places where restricted codes are used by subcultures, at the level of intragenerational stratifications. Beyond these contexts, they create differences and divisions.

Remediations, which form the new type of nature and are the basic glue of the communities in which we now participate, as well as the main factors which differentiate them, have another enormously important implication: they accelerate the processes of mediamorphosis. (see Fidler, 1997). The result of mediamorphosis is the integration of various forms of communication into a single device (most usually an internet-connected computer or phone). **The compiling of bundles of different types of content in a single screen, and managing them through the use of a single interface, leads to a growing intimacy of content perception, which used to be experienced communally (television, radio, music). Through this, bonds which used to be based on physical proximity, group participation and experience in the context of media experiences are being disvalued. This signifies the "expiration" of certain consumption situations, which until recently were synonymous with human relations with media. These situations include sitting on the couch and watching television, listening to music from a dedicated device, or watching rented movies. Their "expiration" does not mean that these situations no longer occur, or that they've been completely erased from social consciousness, but they have become unusual, unique and uncommon. Individuals participate in them with full awareness of their old-fashioned nature, and the fact that they have been replaced by new forms of consuming culture – which have become dominant.** These new devices separate individuals in the process of media consumption, making it highly egotistical and intimate, while also creating new forms of relations: creating communities based on interests and fascinations. These communities, which are not located in a specific space and whose members are scattered, are connected by strong communal bonds. The traditional model of media consumption activity was centered on the object-medium, a device which drew individuals to it and generated bonds based on physical proximity and the mutual experiences of reactions and emotions. Today's media-objects isolate individuals while creating bonds based on shared interests and fascinations. The delocalization of communities problematizes the role of the material aspect of a bond's origin, but does not delete it. Media-objects are no longer apartments, furniture, statues, architecture or television sets – containers or condensers of the social world whose unchangeability expressed the stability of a community and objectified its existence. Today, they play a more fundamental function – they allow the existence of communities which lack sensory outputs, are more scattered and whose membership is more fluid, while remaining stable as a unique connection between humans and objects. The obviousness of these media objects for younger generations makes them the subject of an experiment on life without fundaments but within a communalized network created by people and machines in a state of permanent connection to means of communication.

To study and understand the young, we must consider this new existential situation, which is qualitatively different from the one whose source was the hard and unchanging materiality of reality, which, on one hand, limited us while providing stability, support and security.

Marek Krajewski

In this last chapter, along with invited experts, we pose new questions about cultural participation. We decided to carry out an ethnographic study and shape our project in a "fieldwork" frame, so that along with our collaborators and cultural and social scientists, we could create a new set of questions which are more relevant to a new cultural environment mediated by digital networked technologies.

Żuku, who was profiled at the beginning of this chapter, provides appropriate closure to the discussions we carried out in this report (sharing of digital media as a new, "multiplying" form of cultural content, the identity building component of cultural consumption and creativity, enthusiasm as an organizing force in cultural participation). He is also a great introduction into a different discussion, illustrating the difficulty of determining who is today's "consumer of culture"? Not only do we not know how to operationalize the term "consumer" – we also struggle (along with Wiesław Godzic, Wojciech J. Burszta and Marek Krajewski) to say just what is this new "culture." Posing more precise questions will help us articulate this problem.

One of the fundamental questions is determining the limits of culture – what is and what isn't culture. This is related to culturalization (the growing significance of various cultural content in individuals' self-development and the transfer of many critical conflicts and choices from the social sphere into the cultural one), changes in the role played by cultural institutions as well as evolving boundaries of the private and public. As Wiesław Godzic wrote, it is no longer necessary to put on a coat and tie and enter into a public space to interact with culture. Thanks to new technologies, culture has become domesticated (or at least domesticable), which as Godzic notes following David Morley – does not mean that it does not leave the home. This further complicates the relations of what is public and what is private.

Questions emerge regarding appropriately evaluating various actions related to culture. Which uses of media and consumption of cultural content are appropriate, which aren't; which are more appropriate and which less so? Małgorzata Jacyno (p. 139) and Wojciech J. Burszta's comments illustrate the complexity of this issue. A simple quantification and categorization of actions is not enough, as one mouse click differs from another. Actions that can at one point be viewed as mindless time-killing, can become an act of creativity in a different context. Watching the same movie can signify different things based on the context – who's watching, why they're watching, what is the person's position within a co-internet, how much will interests, horizons and competencies affect this person's ability to further circulate the cultural content. The cultural object itself becomes unstable: a metacultural approach reveals its evolution through comments, links, materialized connections, JPEG or mp3 files.

How should we discuss culture at a time when it is becoming de-institutionalized, or at least detached from traditional institutions in favor of newer types? Examples of these new "online institutions" which are so significant to young people include YouTube, Digart or Nasza-klasa. The perform various functions, but are important and lively points of reference for today's youth. They are also actively co-created by the young: their shape is a function of numerous uses. How these institutions appear and act is a dynamic and constantly unstable effect of the tensions between a culturally-oriented identity logic – and, as Burszta notes in "insert identity" – the uniqueness of new technologies for which culture is a collection of easily transferred and modified files.

We must consider the phenomenon of being connected and online and the resulting thesis of the inability to separate cultural circulation from identity-creation processes. If communication technologies favor immediacy, codependency and a-hierarchical community consumption/prosumerism and creativity, and modern identities seek an authentic "self" and resonate with these cultural forms which are able to bring people closer in the process of these searches – what is the future of traditional cultural policy which is based on distanced relations of "dissemination" and "teaching" and the stability of "institutions" and "works of art"?

The young people we worked with, are connected with each other on multiple levels; living in a world of networked technologies they are also constantly online. Within their web horizons they have the world and culture at their fingertips. We're suggesting that even though they are invisible at first glance, new media help create the space where young people meet, they mediate their relations and help them understand themselves as well as aid in the fulfillment of their passions in ways that are significantly different than was the case in the "analog" era. This area of contacts, is at the same time the venue for circulating cultural content. Thus both the individual and the cultural environment in which he lives, creates, express himself and communicates with others. Cultural content, in its digital form, circulates in techno-social networks, becoming one of the main tools of social communications. This includes both content created by others, which, in networked circulation, becomes loaded with comments and meta-information, as well as personally created content (most frequently of a visual form).

We noticed that young people are not only consumers of images, they are also their creators and, very frequently, their objects (posing for each others' photographs). One need not be an active creator to participate in this unique image culture which has become a hallmark of the digital era. As we've shown, transferability is a fundamental modality in this world. The images themselves, as well as individuals want to send and receive them. The mechanisms of gift exchange are livened up and gain new significance in a nonmaterial digital world. This circulation is also the basic infrastructure of identity creation. Communications materialized and archived online, are inexorably attached to the exchange of cultural content, knowledge and recommendations, and allow individuals to build their own "self" and negotiate their relations with the world. They also allow for the development of passions and interests and participation in communities of practices in which the desire for togetherness is tied to the exchange of knowledge, and sharing of cultural artifacts is part of the catalogue of possibilities related to creating the "self."

It is significant that the most frequently mentioned actors in these networks are technologies and their users. Institutions participate in these networks only sporadically. Our collaborators are citizens of a net society – which does not only mean communities grouped around information exchange and new communication technologies – but a society in which the network is a basic model of social relations. Both humans and communication technologies are the nexuses of these networks. The relations which we describe in this report are not merely social ones, they are of a techno-social nature. While phones, computers or cameras do not create new relations and situations on their own, without them, these connections would not be possible. The world we are describing is constantly created by people and technologies, which can become actors *sui generis*, allowing the creation of certain practices while disallowing others.

This is why we believe our primary task is finding a language to describe these new socio-cultural phenomena. This would bridge the gap between media studies which focus on affordances provided by communication technologies and ethnography which is traditionally focused on people. If we were to focus only on the media, we would bypass significant practices such as using technologies with similar capabilities for two separate purposes (for example, Skype and Gadu-Gadu, which are similar on a technological level, but the former is overwhelmingly used for long-distance voice communication, while the latter, which also allows audio connections, is almost exclusively used for text communication). It is virtually impossible to separate out technological influences from the practices which we observed. We are describing a world in which computers and the forms which they provide for cultural content (some forms are less successful because they are not optimized for network architecture) are not merely tools in the hands of individuals, but have the potential to gain agency. Our ethnographic research among our collaborators leads us to believe that we are not simply describing people who use technologies, but a world of collective actors – of human and non-human actors. "Socialized body and socialized objects do not belong to separate worlds. They are one, the same *universum*. As body and objects become one, habits gain their full power. They transmit social memory. The successfully create the structure of individual behaviors." (Kaufmann, 2004: 171)

The appearance of computers is clearly the main cause for this change – computers are the basic digital medium which Bolter and Grusin call "remediation machines," while the internet is an informational channel which can be used to transfer any media. Lev Manovich, in describing digital media (internet, computer games, digital photos – everything that is "readable" by a computer) listed cultural transcoding as the most significant effect of the computerization of media, more so than numerical representation, modularity, automatization and variation. "Since new media is created on computers, distributed via computers, stored and archived on computers, the logic of a computer can be expected to have significant influence on the traditional cultural logic of media. That is, we may expect that the computer layer will affect the cultural layer. (...) The result of this composite is the new computer culture: a blend of human and computer meanings, of traditional ways human culture modeled the world and computer's own ways to represent it" (Manovich, 2001: 46).

Our report shows that in writing about the influence of the "computer layer" on culture, we can abandon the conditional tense. The technologies we use have an effect on how we choose, store and create cultural content – this is clear in the daily practices described in the report. This transformation of content is less and less dependent on writing – our research reflects the increasing importance of images. However, this does not mean that text is not significant. It is present, usually as hypertext – which reflects digital media logic – since our collaborators generally view books as a reservoir of consecrated culture, useful only rarely and mostly within a school context. Many of the practices popular among the teenagers participating in our study are related to avoiding traditional hierarchies and methods of formal learning – reflecting the internet's technical architecture. The basis of the global computer network is the E2E (end-to-end) model, which allows a free transfer of content between distant points in the network. Communications that make rounds on the web are not filtered. Thanks to this, the peer-to-peer model of distribution can flourish where the technological separation between broadcasters who make content available and those who download/consume is eliminated. (Our collaborators used peer-to-peer networks to exchange files, but also in communities grouped around services such as Digart, where technological equality translates into a partnership model for didactic relations.)

Individuals and groups have become more significant. Institutions, whose power is not related to their position in circulation networks but rather on a pre-digital inheritance, have declined. Of course, this does not mean that cultural centers and cinemas are losing importance – replaced by peer-to-peer exchange networks or YouTube – such a conclusion would be simplistic and at odds with our theory of the primacy of physical space over remediated contacts. At the same time, the mere possession of a bricks-and-mortar location and official sanctioning, does not allow these institutions to exert a real influence on young people's cultural choices. Thanks to the internet, these young people are probably the most culturally self-sufficient generation in history.

All of these phenomena point to the fact that the world we described in this report is increasingly escaping old categorizations – it is not surprising that in the digital world, multiplying is the result of sharing. Young people's practices cannot be reduced to simple binary opposites. Separating the technological from human, the remediated from the direct; the cultural from the everyday and social is not only difficult or impossible, but actually harmful. We make this claim aware of its consequences, and as such a new perspective is now becoming challenging for cultural participation studies – how does one capture the entire spectrum of activity between mere consumption and creation? Based on our field research this approach appears to be the only viable one – without artificially drawn analytical boundaries.

The clear need for researchers to consider the broad dimensions of the cultural environment means looking not only at the circulation of cultural content and identity-creation processes, but also a new analysis of the resulting new relations and joints which connect the network. We are connected through strong and weak bonds, new technologies strengthen our connection to those close to us, and allow long-distance contact. This contact is not only with people, but also with objects, machines and software. These human-technological hybrids must be considered when questioning culture, as hybrid theory fundamentally alters the current understanding of agency – and as Zygmunt Bauman notes, it is individuals' agency which is at stake, not only in cultural studies, but also in cultural policies.

(SEE)

The photos i took in Ziemielin, Parna and Zahaczewo during the last days of summer in 2009 are neither a document about "youth and media," nor an attempt to illustrate the report. They are simply my effort to interpret a small part of these high school students' world. They all took part in the study and agreed to enter into a 'complex game featuring a camera' with me. The effect of this game is a shared story. I would like it to be considered along with the report, as a visual footnote.

Tomek Ratter

(see)

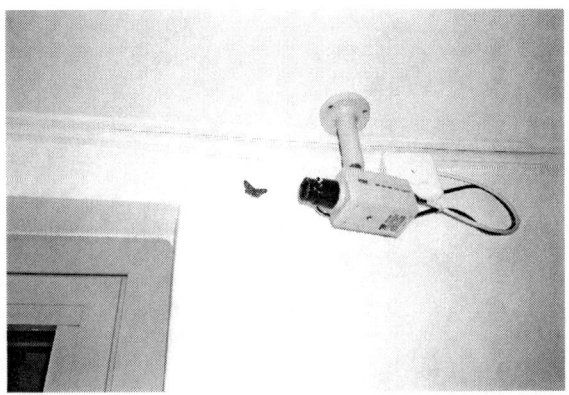

(see)

(see)

(see)

(see)

(see)

(see) 203

(see) 205

(see)

(see)

(see)

Acknowledgments

This report would not exist if it was not for our young collaborators who agreed to take part in the research project, and invited us into their world.

Thank You Very Much.

Additional thanks to:

Tomasz Jędrkiewicz and Robert Zydel for sharing their ethnographic research experiences, and participating in preliminary seminars.

Piotr Toczyski for making study results available and for participation in preliminary seminars.

4P research mix Sp. z o.o. for lending tools and help with recruitment and friendliness.

Teachers and cultural managers who took part in a series of interviews held in July 2009 in Warsaw. They allowed us to prepare our study.

Anna Wieczorek from National Center for Culture (NCK) for her support.

Michał Banasiak, Magda Klimaszewska and Natalia Piesio from the Scientific Research Office of the University of Social Sciences and Humanities in Warsaw for their help and patience.

Polskie Badania Internetu for making data available for analysis.

Commentators: Zygmunt Bauman, Wojciech J. Burszta, José van Dijck, Wiesław Godzic, Małgorzata Jacyno, Henry Jenkins, Marek Krajewski, Mirosława Marody and Tomasz Szkudlarek for texts which inspire us to further work.

Edwin Bendyk, Marta Klimowicz, Grzegorz D. Stunża, Roch Sulima and Alek Tarkowski for their help and support.

The Youth and Media team

Mateusz Halawa for his help during the preparation of the English version of this book.

Mirosław Filiciak

Bibliography

Abriszewski K. (2008). Poznanie, zbiorowość, polityka. Analiza teorii aktora sieci Bruno Latoura, Kraków.
Appadurai A. (1996). Modernity at Large, Minneapolis.
Ascott R. (2003). Telematic Embrace: Visionary Theories of Art, Technology, and Consciousness, London.
Beck U. (2002). *Zombie Categories: Interview with Ulrich Beck*, U. Beck, E. Beck-Gernsheim (eds.), Individualization, London..
Bokszański Z., Piotrowski A., Ziółkowski M. (1977). Socjologia języka, Warszawa.
Bolter J.D., R. Grusin (2000). Remediation: Understanding New Media, Cambridge, MA.
Bourdieu P. (1990). *Fieldwork in Philosophy*, Bourdieu, In Other Words, Stanford.
Burszta, Fatyga et al (2010), Kultura miejska w Polsce z perspektywy interdyscyplinarnych badań jakościowych, Warszawa.
Couldry N. (2004). Theorising media as practice, „Social Semiotics", 14:2, s. 115-132.
Czapiński J. (2009). Polska smuta. Rozmowa z prof. Januszem Czapińskim o kryzysie zaufania, nepotyzmie oraz dobrym i złym kapitale społecznym, „Polityka", nr 2701 z 18.04.2009, pp. 18–20.
Derrida J. (1992). Given Time. I. Counterfeit money, Chicago.
van Dijck J. (2007). Mediated memories in the digital age, Stanford.
Eriksen E. (2001). Tyranny of the moment, London.
Fatyga B. (2001). Normalność i normalka. Próba zastosowania pojęcia normalności do badań młodzieży,Warszawa.
Foucault M. (2000). *Techniki siebie*, Filozofia, historia, polityka. Wybór pism, Warszawa.
Foucault M. (2001). Fearless speech, New York.
Fidler R.F. (1997). Mediamorphosis: Understanding New Media, London.
Giles J. (2005). Internet encyclopaedias go head to head, „Nature", vol. 438, nr 7070, pp. 900–901.
Gleick J. (2000). Faster: the acceleration of just about everything, London.
Granovetter M. (1973). The strength of weak ties, „American Journal of Sociology", 73, s. 1360–1380.
Halawa M. (2007). Od kultury nie ma ucieczki, „Gazeta Wyborcza", 26.07.2007.
Ito M. et al (2008). Living and Learning with New Media: Summary of Findings from the Digital Youth Project, http://digitalyouth.ischool.berkeley.edu/report
Jacyno M. (2007). Kultura indywidualizmu, Warszawa.
Jenkins H. (2006). Convergence Culture, New York.
Kaufman J.C. (2004). Ego. Socjologia jednostki, Warszawa.

Krajewski M. (2008). *Motywy przewodnie i przedmioty*, R. Drozdowski, M. Krajewski (red.), Wyobraźnia społeczna. Horyzonty – źródła – dynamika. Uwarunkowania strategii dostosowawczych współczesnego społeczeństwa polskiego – studium socjologiczne, Poznań.

Latour B. (1992). We have never been modern, Cambridge, MA.

Latour B. (2005). Reassembling the Social. An Introduction to Actor-Network Theory, Nowy Jork.

Malinowski B. (2005). Agronauci Zachodniego Pacyfiku, Warszawa.

Mauss M. (2000 [1950]). Szkic o darze. Forma i podstawa wymiany w społeczeństwach archaicznych, „Socjologia i Antropologia", Warszawa.

Marvin C. (1990). When Old Technologies Were New: Thinking About Electric Communication in the Late Nineteenth Century, Oxford.

Mitchel W.J.T. (2005). There Are No Visual Media, „Journal of Visual Culture", vol. 4(2), pp. 257–266.

Magala S. (1999). Między giełdą a śmietnikiem. Eseje simmlowskie, Gdańsk.

Manovich L. (2008). The Practice of Everyday (Media) Life, http://www.egs.edu/faculty/lev-manovich/articles/the-practice-of-everyday-media-life/

Manovich L. (2001). The Language of New Media, Cambridge, MA.

Morley D. (2003). Być w domu w mobilnym świecie, „Kultura Popularna", nr 3(5)/2003.

Shirky C. (2009). A Speculative Post on the Idea of Algorithmic Authority, http://www.shirky.com/weblog/2009/11/a-speculative-post-on-the-idea-of-algorithmic-authority

Simmel G. (2006). *Socjologia zmysłów*, Simmel, Most i drzwi, Warszawa.

Szarecki A. (2009). *Last.fm. Statystyka tożsamości*, M. Filiciak, G. Ptaszek (eds.), Komunikowanie (się) w mediach elektronicznych – język, semiotyka, Warszawa, pp. 343–359.

Urban G. (2001). Metaculture: How Cultures Move through the World, Minnesota.

Wellman B., Hogan B. (2004). The Internet in Everyday Life, http://chass.utoronto.ca/~wellman/publications/inet_everyday/

Wenger E. (1998). Communities of Practice. Learning, Meaning and Identity, Cambridge.

Wenger E. (2006). Communities of Practice. A Brief Introduction, http://www.ewenger.com/theory/communities_of_practice_intro.htm

Żulczyk J. (2008). Radio Armageddon, Warszawa.

Notes on contributors

Zygmunt Bauman – sociologist, emeritus professor at the University of Leeds. His most recent books include *Culture in a Liquid Modern World* and *This is Not a Diary*.

Wojciech J. Burszta – cultural anthropologist, professor of cultural studies at the Warsaw School of Social Sciences and Humanities.

Michał Danielewicz – sociologist, collaborator of Centrum Cyfrowe think-and-do tank. Ethnographer in the "Youth and Media" project and co-author of this book.

Mirosław Filiciak – media studies professor at the Warsaw School of Social Sciences and Humanities and the head of research departament of the Centrum Cyfrowe. The leader of "Youth and media" project, co-author of this book.

Wiesław Godzic – media scholar, professor of cultural studies at the Warsaw School of Social Sciences and Humanities.

Aleksandra Gołdys – sociologist, ethnographer in "Youth and Media" project.

Mateusz Halawa – doctoral candidate at the New School for Social Research and University of Warsaw, co-author of this book.

Małgorzata Jacyno – sociologist, professor at the Institute of Sociology of the University of Warsaw.

Henry Jenkins – Provost's Professor of Communication, Journalism, and Cinematic Arts at the University of Southern California. He is co-author of *Spreadable Media: Creating Meaning and Value in a Networked Culture*.

Paulina Jędrzejewska – social researcher, ethnographer in "Youth and Media" project, author of the accompanying documentary film

Marek Krajewski – sociologist, professor at the Sociology Institute of Adam Mickiewicz University in Poznań.

Mirosława Marody – professor of social psychology at the Institute of Sociology at the University of Warsaw and the vice-president of the Polish Academy of Sciences.

Paweł Mazurek – sociologist and business coach, ethnographer in "Youth and Media" project and co-author of this book.

Agata Nowotny – doctoral candidate at the Institute of Sociology at the University of Warsaw. A coordinator of "Youth and Media" project and co-author of this book.

Tomek Ratter – studied at Opava School of Photography, a photographer in "Youth and Media" project.

Agnieszka Strzemińska – sociologist, studied at University of Warsaw. Ethnographer in "Youth and Media" project.

Jacek Szejda – programming sociologist, works at Educational Research Institute in Warsaw. Ethnographer in "Youth and Media" project.

Tomasz Szkudlarek – professor at University of Gdansk, where he chairs Department of Philosophy of Education and Cultural Studies in Institute of Education, Faculty of Social Sciences.

José van Dijck – professor of Comparative Media Studies at the University of Amsterdam. She is the author of *Mediated Memories in the Digital Age*.

Warsaw Studies in Culture and Society

Edited by Jacek Wasilewski

Vol. 1 Magdalena Góra / Zdzisław Mach / Katarzyna Zielińska: Collective Identity and Democracy in the Enlarging Europe. 2012.

Vol. 2 Paula Bialski: Becoming Intimately Mobile. 2012.

Vol. 3 Mirosław Filiciak / Michał Danielewicz / Mateusz Halawa / Paweł Mazurek / Agata Nowotny: Youth and Media. New Media and Cultural Participation. 2013.

www.peterlang.de